THE

MAGUS,

OR

CELESTIAL INTELLIGENCER;

BEING

A COMPLETE SYSTEM OF

OCCULT PHILOSOPHY.

———

IN THREE BOOKS:

Containing the Antient and Modern Practice of the Cabaliftic Art, Natural and Celeftial Magic, &c.; fhewing the wonderful Effects that may be performed by a Knowledge of the

Celestial Influences, the occult Properties of Metals, Herbs, and Stones,

AND THE

APPLICATION OF ACTIVE TO PASSIVE PRINCIPLES.

EXHIBITING

THE SCIENCES OF NATURAL MAGIC;

Alchymy, or Hermetic Philosophy;

ALSO

THE NATURE CREATION, AND FALL OF MAN;

His natural and fupernatural Gifts; the magical Power inherent in the Soul, &c:; with a great Variety of rare Experiments in Natural Magic:

THE CONSTELLATORY PRACTICE, or TALISMANIC MAGIC;

The Nature of the Elements, Stars, Planets, Signs, &c.; the Conftruction and Compofition of all Sorts of Magic Seals, Images, Rings, Glaffes, &c.;

The Virtue and Efficacy of Numbers, Characters, and Figures, of good and evil Spirits.

MAGNETISM,

AND CABALISTICAL OR CEREMONIAL MAGIC;

In which the fecret Myfteries of the Cabala are explained; the Operations of good and evil Spirits; all Kinds of Cabaliftic Figures, Tables, Seals, and Names, with their Ufe, &c.

THE TIMES, BONDS, OFFICES, AND CONJURATION OF SPIRITS.

TO WHICH IS ADDED

Biographia Antiqua, or the Lives of the most eminent Philosophers, Magi, &c.

The Whole illustrated with a great Variety of

CURIOUS ENGRAVINGS, MAGICAL AND CABALISTICAL FIGURES, &c.

———

BY FRANCIS BARRETT, F.R.C.

Professor of Chemistry, natural and occult Philosophy, the Cabala, &c. &c.

LONDON:

PRINTED FOR LACKINGTON, ALLEN, AND CO., TEMPLE OF THE MUSES, FINSBURY SQUARE.

1801.

The Magus: Book 1
ISBN 1-58509-031-X

Also Available:

The Magus: Book 2
ISBN 1-58509-032-8

The Magus: The Set
ISBN 1-58509-033-6

Published by
The Book Tree
Post Office Box 724
Escondido, CA 92033

Call (800) 700-TREE for a FREE BOOK TREE CATALOG with over 1000 Books, Booklets, Audio, and Video on Alchemy, Ancient Mysteries, Anti-Gravity, Atlantis, Free Energy, Gnosticism, Health Issues, Magic, Metaphysics, Mythology, Occult, Rare Books, Religious Controversy, Sitchin Studies, Spirituality, Symbolism, Tesla, and much more. Or visit our website at www.thebooktree.com

Orme Del. & Sculp. Engraver to the King &c.

Francis Barrett

Student in Chemistry, Metaphysicks,

Natural & Occult Philosophy &c. &c.

THE MAGUS: BOOK ONE

INTRODUCTION TO BOOK ONE

The Magus has proved to be the most sought after set of books on magic and alchemy ever published. There is very good reason for this. These books are powerful, and were considered so dangerous that for many years, rare copies could only be found in certain libraries, locked away from the general public and from those who would use (or misuse) its power.

The original set of books was first published in 1801 by its author, Francis Barrett, who first spent many years of diligent study before releasing them. His premise for the material, that is, before putting anything into these books, Barrett first subjected the various theories to certain tests that had to be "substantiated by nature, truth, and experiment" first. In other words, the magical practices had to work on a convincing level before Barrett would bother including them. Anything that he considered interesting, but idle speculation, was discounted and not included.

The first half of Book One covers what Barrett refers to as Natural Magic. This is "magic" which, when done in such a way, will produce its effects naturally. He includes the secret to alchemy and the philosopher's stone near the end of this section, which I urge one to read and study *carefully*. Barrett's detailed experiments, which prove these natural effects, are also included in this section. He cautions, however, that attempting to understand the results may be futile. Just understand that the principles work—and be careful!

This goes double for Part Two, which gets into Talismanic Magic. If someone should devote oneself to this section and practice with set goals and clear intent, it is quite certain they will come away completely convinced of certain powers beyond the human realm. This section clearly shows how talismans are made and how they work; how and why astral spirits become involved, and how and why magic is meant for goodness rather than evil. Barrett also shows in this section the power of numbers and mathematical formulas, plus reveals a number of magical seals, mostly from Agrippa and Paracelsus, which use these said formulas.

This information is not to be used as a toy. It is not a joke. It is spiritually based research—some of which makes little sense on a logical or practical level—but in many cases it works. Concentration and good intentions are essential elements for success, and people embarking on this "journey" should not consider it lightly and jump in and "play around." Although outer results may be apparent, this is inner work. If not done properly, meaning if these things are not done with good intent, it will "mess you up" because one will otherwise be attracting elements (or elementals) that do not have good intentions in mind. We all have good and bad within each of us, and the surrounding spirit world is not outside of this general rule. Just because something cannot be seen, doesn't mean that it is completely unable to jump up and bite you in the you know where, if you start poking at it. In other words, do not misuse these books. Treat them with the respect they deserve. If you do, certain things may well manifest which will show respect to you.

Paul Tice

PREFACE.

———◇◇◇———

IN this Work, which we have written chiefly for the information of those who are curious and indefatigable in their enquiries into occult knowledge, we have, at a vast labour and expence, both of time and charges, collected whatsoever can be deemed curious and rare, in regard to the subject of our speculations in Natural Magic---the Cabala---Celestial and Ceremonial Magic---Alchymy---and Magnetism; and have divided it into two Books, sub-divided into Parts: to which we have added a third Book, containing a biographical account of the lives of those great men who were famous and renowned for their knowledge; shewing upon whose authority this Science of Magic is founded, and upon what principles. To which we have annexed a great variety of notes, wherein we have impartially examined the probability of the existence of *Magic*, both of the good and bad species, in the earliest, as well as in the latter, ages of the world. We have exhibited a vast number of rare experiments in the course of this Treatise, many of which, delivered in the beginning, are founded upon the simple application of actives to passives; the others are of a higher speculation.

In our history of the lives of Philosophers, &c. we have omitted nothing that can be called interesting or satisfactory. We have taken our historical characters from those authors most deserving of credit; we have given an outline of the various reports tradition gives of them; to which are annexed notes, drawn from the most probable appearance of truth, impartially describing their characters and actions; leaning neither to the side of those who doubt every thing, nor to them whose credulity takes in every report to be circumstantially true.

At

At this time, the abstruse sciences of Nature begin to be more investigated than for a century past, during which space they have been almost totally neglected; but men becoming more enlightened, they begin to consider the extraordinary effects that were wrought by ancient philosophers, in ages that were called dark. Many, therefore, have thought that time, nature, causes, and effects, being the same, with the additional improvements of mechanical and liberal arts, we may, with *their knowledge of Nature*, surpass them in the producing of wonderful effects; for which cause many men are naturally impelled, without education or other advantage, to dive into the contemplation of Nature; but the study thereof being at first difficult, they have recourse to lay out a great deal of money in collecting various books : to remedy which inconvenience and expence, the Author undertook to compose THE MAGUS, presuming that his labours herein will meet with the general approbation of either the novitiate or adept : for whose use and instruction it is now published.

But to return to the subject of our Book : we have, in the First Part, fully explained what Natural Magic is; and have shewn that, by the application of actives to passives, many wonderful effects are produced that are merely natural, and done by manual operations. We have procured every thing that was valuable and scarce respecting this department of our work, which we have introduced under the title of Natural Magic; and a variety of our own experiments likewise. In the possession of this work, the laborious and diligent student will find a complete and delectable companion; so that he who has been searching for years, for this author and the other, will in this book find the marrow of them all.

But I would advise, that we do not depend too much upon *our own wisdom* in the understanding of these mysteries; for all earthly wisdom is foolishness in the esteem of God---I mean all the wisdom of man, which he pretends to draw from any other source than God alone.

We come next to the Second Part of our First Book, treating of the art called the *Constellatory Practice*, or *Talismanic Magic;* in which we fully demonstrate the power and efficacy of *Talismans*, so much talked of, and so little understood,

understood, by most men : we therefore explain, in the clearest and most intelligible manner, how *Talismans* may be made, for the execution of various
purposes, and by what means, and from what source they become vivified, and
are visible instruments of great and wonderful effects. We likewise shew the
proper and convenient times ; under what constellations and aspects of the
planets they are to be formed, and the times when they are most powerful to
act ; and, in the next place, we have taught that our own spirit is the vehicle
of celestial attraction, transferring celestial and spiritual virtue into *Seals,
Images, Amulets, Rings, Papers, Glasses, &c.* Also, we have not forgot to give
the most clear and rational illustration of sympathy and antipathy---attraction
and repulsion. We have likewise proved how cures are performed by virtue
of sympathetic powers and medicines---by seals, rings, and amulets, even at
unlimited distances, which we have been witnesses of and are daily confirmed
in the true and certain belief of. We know how to communicate with any
person, and to give him intimation of our purpose, at a hundred or a thousand
miles distance ; but then a preparation is necessary, and the parties should
have their appointed seasons and hours for that purpose ; likewise, both should
be of the same firm constancy of mind, and a disciple or brother in art.
And we have given methods whereby a man may receive true and certain
intimation of future things (by dreams), of whatsoever his mind has before
meditated upon, himself being properly disposed. Likewise, we have recited
the various methods used by the antients for the invocation of astral spirits,
by *circles, crystals, &c. ;* their forms of exorcism, incantations, orations, bonds,
conjurations ; and have given a general display of the instruments of their
art ; all of which we have collected out of the works of the most famous
magicians, such as Zoroaster, Hermes, Apollonius, Simon of the Temple,
Trithemius, Agrippa, Porta (the Neapolitan), Dee, Paracelsus, Roger Bacon,
and a great many others ; to which we have subjoined our own notes, endea-
vouring to point out the difference of these arts, so as to free the name of Magic
from any scandalous imputation ; seeing it is a word originally significative
not of any evil, but of every good and laudable science, such as a man might
profit by, and become both wise and happy ; and the practice so far from
being

being offensive to God or man, that the very root or ground of all magic takes its rise from the Holy Scriptures, viz.---"The fear of God is the beginning of all wisdom;"---and charity is the end : which fear of God is the beginning of Magic; for Magic is wisdom, and on this account the wise men were called *Magi*. The magicians were the first Christians; for, by their high and excellent knowledge, they knew that that Saviour which was promised, was now born man---that Christ was our Redeemer, Advocate, and Mediator; they were the first to acknowledge his glory and majesty; therefore let no one be offended at the venerable and sacred title of Magician---a title which every wise man merits while he pursues that path which Christ himself trod, viz. humility, charity, mercy, fasting, praying, &c.; for the true magician is the truest Christian, and nearest disciple of our blessed Lord, who set the example we ought to follow; for he says---"If ye have faith, &c.;" and "This kind comes not by fasting and prayer, &c.;" and "Ye shall tread upon scorpions, &c.;" and again, "Be wise as serpents, and harmless as doves."---Such instructions as these are frequently named, and given in many places of the Holy Scriptures. Likewise, all the Apostles confess the power of working miracles through faith in the name of Christ Jesus, and that all wisdom is to be attained through him; for he says, "I am the light of the world!"

We have thought it adviseable, likewise, to investigate the power of numbers, their sympathy with the divine names of God; and, seeing the whole universe was created by number, weight, and measure, there is no small efficacy in numbers, because nothing more clearly represents the Divine Essence to human understanding than numbers; seeing that in all the Divine holy names there is still a conformity of numbers, so that the conclusion of this our First Book forms a complete system of mathematical magic; in which I have collected a vast number of curious seals from that famous magician Agrippa, and likewise from Paracelsus, noting them particularly, as I have found them correspondent with true science on experiment.

The Second Book forms a complete treatise on the mysteries of the Cabala and Ceremonial Magic; by the study of which, a man (who can separate himself from material objects, by the mortification of the sensual appetite---

abstinence

abstinence from drunkenness, gluttony, and other bestial passions, and who lives pure and temperate, free from those actions which degenerate a man to a brute) may become a recipient of Divine light and knowledge; by which they may foresee things to come, whether to private families, or kingdoms, or states, empires, battles, victories, &c.; and likewise be capable of doing much good to their fellow-creatures : such as the healing of all disorders, and assisting with the comforts of life the unfortunate and distressed.

We have spoken largely of prophetic dreams and visions in our Cabalistic Magic, and have given the tables of the Cabala, fully set down for the information of the wise ; some few most secret things being reserved by the Author for his pupils only, not to be taught by publication.

The Third Book forms a complete Magical Biography, being collected from most antient authors, and some scarce and valuable manuscripts ; and which has been the result of much labour in acquiring. Therefore, those who wish to benefit in those studies, must shake off the drowsiness of worldly vanity, all idle levity, sloth, intemperance, and lust ; so that they may be quiet, clean, pure, and free from every distraction and perturbation of mind, and worthily use the knowledge he obtains from his labours.

Therefore, my good friend, whosoever thou art, that desirest to accomplish these things, be but persuaded first to apply thyself to the ETERNAL WISDOM, entreating him to grant thee understanding, then seeking knowledge with diligence, and thou shalt never repent thy having taken so laudable a resolution, but thou shalt enjoy a secret happiness and serenity of mind, which the world can never rob thee of.

Wishing thee every success imaginable in thy studies and experiments, hoping that thou wilt use the benefits that thou mayest receive to the honour of our Creator and for the profit of thy neighbour, in which exercise thou shalt ever experience the satisfaction of doing thy duty ; remember our instructions--- to be silent : talk only with those worthy of thy communication---do not give pearls to swine ; be friendly to all, but not familiar with all ; for many are, as the Scriptures mention---wolves in sheep clothing.

FRANCIS BARRETT.

TABLE OF CONTENTS.

CHAP.

BOOK II.----PART I.

CHAP.

DIREC·

DIRECTIONS FOR PLACING THE PLATES.

—

BOOK I.

BOOK II.

ADVERTISEMENT.

As an Introduction to the Study of Natural Magic, we have thought fit to premise a short discourse on the Influence of the Stars, and on Natural Magic in general, showing how far the influences of the heavenly bodies are useful to our purposes, and likewise to what extent we may admit those influences; rejecting some speculations concerning the planetary inclinations, as far as they appertain to questionary abuses, that seem to us idle, and of no validity, or yet founded on any principles of sound philosophy, or corresponding to the word of God in the Scriptures. In which discourse we have fully set down our reasons for rejecting some parts of astrology, and admitting others which are founded on good principles, and coinciding with the Scriptures and Natural Philosophy: our purpose being to clear the understanding of errors, and not to enforce any thing but what appears to be substantiated by nature, truth, and experiment.

INTRO-

INTRODUCTION

STUDY OF NATURAL MAGIC.

OF THE INFLUENCES OF THE STARS.

I T has been a subject of ancient dispute whether or not
the stars, as second causes, do so rule and influence man as to ingraft in his
nature certain passions, virtues, propensities, &c., and this to take root in him
at the very critical moment of his being born into this vale of misery and
wretchedness ; likewise, if their site and configuration at this time do shew
forth his future passions and pursuits ; and by their revolutions, transits, and
directed aspects, they point out the particular accidents of the body, marriage,
sickness, preferments, and such like ; the which I have often revolved in my
mind for many years past, having been at all times in all places a warm
advocate for stellary divination or astrology : therefore in this place it is highly
necessary that we examine how far this influence extends to man, seeing that I
fully admit that man is endowed with a free-will from God, which the stars
can in no wise counteract. And as there is in man the power and apprehension
of all divination, and wonderful things, seeing that we have a complete system
in ourselves, therefore are we called the microcosm, or little world ; for we carry

a heaven

a heaven in ourselves from our beginning, for God hath sealed in us the image of himself; and of all created beings we are the epitome, therefore we must be careful, lest we confound and mix one thing with another.   Nevertheless, man, as a pattern of the great world, sympathizes with it according to the stars, which, agreeably to the Holy Scriptures, are set for times and seasons, and not as causes of this or that evil, which may pervade kingdoms or private families, although they do in some measure foreshew them, yet they are in no wise the cause; therefore I conceive in a wide different sense to what is generally understood that " Stars rule men, but a *wise man* rules the stars :" to which I answer, that the stars do not rule men, according to the vulgar and received opinion ; as if the stars should stir up men to murders, seditions, broils, lusts, fornications, adulteries, drunkenness, &c., which the common astrologers hold forth as sound and true doctrine ; because, they say, Mars and Saturn, being conjunct, do this and much more, and many other configurations and afflictions of the two great infortunes *(as they are termed)*, when the benevolent planets Jupiter, Venus, and Sol, happen to be detrimented or afflicted ; therefore, then, they say men influenced by them are most surely excited to the commission of the vices before named ; yet a wise man may, by the liberty of his own free-will, make those affections and inclinations void, and this they call " To rule the stars;" but let them know, according to the sense here understood, first, it is not in a wise man to resist evil inclinations, but of the grace of God, and we call none wise but such as are endued with grace ; for, as we have said before, all natural wisdom from the hands of man is foolishness in the sight of God ; which was not before understood to be a wise man fenced with grace ; for why should he rule the stars, who has not any occasion to fear conquered inclinations ?—therefore a natural wise man is as subject to the slavery of sin as others more ignorant than himself, yet the stars do not incline him to sin. God created the heavens without spot, and pronounced them good, therefore it is the greatest absurdity to suppose the stars, by a continual inclining of us to this or that misdeed, should be our tempters, which we eventually make them, if we admit they cause inclinations ; but know that it is not from without, but within, by sin, that evil inclinations do arise : according to the Scriptures,

" Out

" Out of the heart of man proceed evil cogitations, murmurs, adulteries, thefts, murders, &c." Because, as the heavens and apprehension of all celestial virtues are sealed by God in the soul and spirit of man ; so when man becomes depraved by sin and the indulgence of his gross and carnal appetite, he then becomes the seat of the Infernal Powers, which may be justly deemed a hell; for then the bodily and fleshly sense obscures the bright purity and thinness of the spirit, and he becomes the instrument of our spiritual enemy in the exercise of all infernal lusts and passions.

Therefore it is most necessary for us to know that we are to beware of granting or believing any effects from the influences of the stars more than they have naturally ; because there are many whom I have lately conversed with, and great men, too, in this nation, who readily affirm that the *stars* are the causes of any kinds of diseases, inclinations, and fortunes ; likewise that they blame the stars for all their misconduct and misfortunes.

Nevertheless, we do not by these discourses prohibit or deny all influence to the stars ; on the contrary, we affirm there is a natural sympathy and antipathy amongst all things throughout the whole universe, and this we shall shew to be displayed through a variety of effects ; and likewise that the stars, as signs, do foreshew great mutations, revolutions, deaths of great men, governors of provinces, kings, and emperors ; likewise the weather, tempests, earthquakes, deluges, &c. ; and this according to the law of Providence. The lots of all men do stand in the hands of the Lord, for he is the end and beginning of all things ; he can remove crowns and sceptres, and displace the most cautious arrangements and councils of man, who, when he thinks himself most secure, tumbles headlong from the seat of power, and lies grovelling in the dust.

Therefore our astrologers in most of their speculations seek without a light, for they conceive every thing may be known or read in the stars ; if an odd silver spoon is but lost, the innocent stars are obliged to give an account of it ; if an old maiden loses a favourite puppy, away she goes to an oracle of divination for information of the whelp. Oh ! vile credulity, to think that those celestial bodies take cognizance of, and give in their configurations and aspects, continual information of the lowest and vilest transactions of dotards, the most

trivial

trivial and frivolous questions that are *pretended* to be resolved by an inspection into the figure of the heavens. Well does our legislature justly condemn as juggling impostors all those idle vagabonds who infest various parts of this metropolis, and impose upon the simple and unsuspecting, by answering, for a shilling or half-crown fee, whatever thing or circumstance may be proposed to them, as if they were God's vicegerents on earth, and his deputed privy counsellors.

They do not even scruple ever to persuade poor mortals of the lower class, that they shew images in glasses, as if they actually confederated with evil spirits : a notable instance I will here recite, that happened very lately in this city. Two penurious Frenchmen, taking advantage of the credulity of the common people, who are continually gaping after such toys, had so contrived a telescope or optic glass as that various letters and figures should be reflected in an obscure manner, shewing the images of men and women, &c. ; so that when any one came to consult these jugglers, after paying the usual fee, they, according to the urgency of the query, produced answers by those figures or letters ; the which affrights the inspector into the glass so much, that he or she supposes they have got some devilish thing or other in hand, by which they remain under the full conviction of having actually beheld the parties they wished to see, though perhaps they may at the same time be residing many hundreds of miles distance therefrom ; they, having received this impression from a pre-conceived idea of seeing the image of their friend in this optical machine, go away, and anon report, with an addition of ten hundred lies, that they have been witness of a miracle. I say this kind of deception is only to be acted with the vulgar, who, rather than have their imaginations balked, would swallow the most abominable lies and conceits. For instance, who would suppose that any rational being could be persuaded that a fellow-creature of proper size and stature should be able by any means to thrust his body into a quart bottle ?—the which thing was advertised to the public by a merry knave (not thinking there were such fools in existence), to be done by him in a public theatre. Upwards of 600 persons were assembled to behold the transaction, never doubting but the fellow meant to keep his word, when to the great mortification

and

and disgrace of this long-headed audience, the conjuror came forth amidst a general stir and buz of "Ay, now! see! now! see! he is just going to jump in."—"Indeed," says the conjuror, "ladies and gentlemen, I am not; for if you were such fools as to believe such an absurdity, I am not wise enough to do it:"—therefore, making his bow, he disappeared, to the great discomfort of these wise-heads, who straightway withdrew in the best manner they could.

As for the telescope magicians, they were taken into custody by the gentlemen of the police office, in Bow Street; nor would their familiar do them the kindness to attempt their rescue.

But to have done with these things that are unworthy our notice as philosophers, and to proceed to matters of a higher nature: it is to be noted what we have before said, in respect of the influences of the stars, that Ptolemy, in his quadrapartite, in speaking of *generals*, comes pretty near our ideas on the subject of planetary influence, of which we did not at any time doubt, but do not admit (nay, it is not necessary, seeing there is an astrology in Nature),—that each action of our life, our afflictions, fortunes, accidents, are deducible to the influential effects of the planets: they proceed from ourselves; but I admit that our thoughts, actions, cogitations, sympathize with the stars upon the principle of general sympathy. Again, there is a much stronger sympathy between persons of like constitution and temperament, for each mortal creature possesses a Sun and system within himself; therefore, according to universal sympathy, we are affected by the general influence or universal spirit of the world, as the vital principle throughout the universe: therefore we are not to look into the configurations of the stars for the cause or incitement of men's bestial inclinations, for brutes have their specifical inclinations from the propagation of their principle by seed, not by the sign of the horoscope; therefore as man is oftentimes capable of the actions and excesses of brutes, they cannot happen to a man naturally from any other source than the seminal being infused in his composition; for seeing likewise that the soul is immortal, and endued with free-will, which acts upon the body, the soul cannot be inclined by any configuration of the stars either to good or evil; but from its own immortal power of willingly being seduced by sin, it prompts to evil; but enlightened by God, it springs to good, on

either

either principle, according to its tendency, the soul feeds while in this frail body; but what further concerns the soul of man in this, and after this, we shall fully investigate the natural magic of the soul, in which we have fully treated every point of enquiry that has been suggested to us by our own imagination, and by scientific experiments have proved its divine virtue originally sealed therein by the Author of its being.

Sufficient it is to return to our subject relative to astrology, especially to know what part of it is necessary for our use, of which we will select that which is pure and to our purpose, for the understanding and effecting of various experiments in the course of our works, leaving the tedious calculation of nativities, the never-ceasing controversies and cavillations of its professors, the dissensions which arise from the various modes of practice; all which we leave to the figure-casting plodder, telling him, by-the-by, that whatever he thinks he can foreshew by inspecting the horoscope of a nativity, by long, tedious, and night-wearied studies and contemplations; I say, whatever he can shew respecting personal or national mutations, changes, accidents, &c. &c., all this we know by a much easier and readier method; and can more comprehensively, clearly, and intelligibly, shew and point out, to the very letter, by our Cabal, which we know to be true, without deviation, juggling, fallacy, or collusion, or any kind of deceit or imposture whatsoever; which Cabal or spiritual astrology we draw from the Fountain of Knowledge, in all simplicity, humility, and truth; and we boast not of ourselves, but of Him who teaches us through his divine mercy, by the light of whose favour we see into things spiritual and divine: in the possession of which we are secure amidst the severest storms of hatred, malice, pride, envy, hypocrisy, levity, bonds, poverty, imprisonment, or any other outward circumstance; we should still be rich, want nothing, be fed with delicious meats, and enjoy plentifully all good things necessary for our support: all this we do not vainly boast of, as figurative, ideal, or chimerical; but real, solid, and everlasting, in the which we exult and delight, and praise his name for ever and ever: Amen.

All which we publicly declare to the world for the honour of our God, being at all times ready to do every kindness we can to our poor neighbour, and,

as

as far as in us lies, to comfort him, sick or afflicted; in doing which we ask no reward : it is sufficient to us that we can do it, and that we may be acceptable to Him who says—" I am the light of the world; to whom with the Father, and Holy Spirit, be ascribed all power, might, majesty, and dominion : Amen."

To the faithful and discreet Student of Wisdom.

Greeting :

TAKE our instructions; in all things ask counsel of God, and he will give it; offer up the following prayer daily for the illumination of thy understanding : depend for all things on God, the first cause; with whom, by whom, and in whom, are all things : see thy first care be to know thyself; and then in humility direct thy prayer as follows.

A Prayer or Oration to God.

ALMIGHTY and most merciful God, we thy servants approach with fear and trembling before thee, and in all humility do most heartily beseech thee to pardon our manifold and blind transgressions, by us committed at any time; and grant, O, most merciful Father, for his sake who died upon the cross, that our minds may be enlightened with the divine radiance of thy holy wisdom ; for seeing, O, Lord of might, power, majesty, and dominion, that, by reason of our gross and material bodies, we are scarce apt to receive those spiritual instructions that we so earnestly and heartily desire. Open, O, blessed Spirit, the spiritual eye of our soul, that we may be released from this darkness overspreading us by the delusions of the outward senses, and may perceive and understand those things which are spiritual. We pray thee, oh, Lord, above all to strengthen our souls and bodies against our

BOOK I.   B   spiritual

spiritual enemies, by the blood and righteousness of our blessed Redeemer, thy Son, Jesus Christ; and through him, and in his name, we beseech thee to illuminate the faculties of our souls, so that we may clearly and comprehensively hear with our ears, and understand with our hearts; and remove far from us all hypocrisy, deceitful dealing, profaneness, inconstancy, and levity; so that we may, in word and act, become thy faithful servants, and stand firm and unshaken against all the attacks of our bodily enemies, and likewise be proof against all illusions of evil spirits, with whom we desire no communication or interest; but that we may be instructed in the knowledge of things, natural and celestial : and as it pleased thee to bestow on Solomon all wisdom, both human and divine; in the desire of which knowledge he did so please thy divine majesty, that in a dream, of one night, thou didst inspire him with all wisdom and knowledge, which he did wisely prefer before the riches of this life; so may our desire and prayer be graciously accepted by thee; so that, by a firm dependence on thy word, we may not be led away by the vain and ridiculous pursuits of worldly pleasures and delights, they not being durable, nor of any account to our immortal happiness. Grant us, Lord, power and strength of intellect to carry on this work, for the honour and glory of thy holy name, and to the comfort of our neighbour ; and without design of hurt or detriment to any, we may proceed in our labours, through Jesus Christ, our Redeemer : Amen.

OF NATURAL MAGIC IN GENERAL.

BEFORE we proceed to particulars, it will not be amiss to speak of generals ; therefore, as an elucidation, we shall briefly show what sciences we comprehend under the title of Natural Magic ; and to hasten to the point, we shall regularly proceed from theory to practice ; therefore, Natural Magic undoubtedly comprehends a knowledge of all Nature, which we by no means can arrive at but by searching deeply into her treasury,

which

which is inexhaustible; we therefore by long study, labour, and practice, have found out many valuable secrets and experiments, which are either unknown, or are buried in the ignorant knowledge of the present age. The wise ancients knew that in Nature the greatest secrets lay hid, and wonderful active powers were dormant, unless excited by the vigorous faculty of the mind of man; but as, in these latter days, men give themselves almost wholly up to vice and luxury, so their understandings have become more and more depraved; 'till, being swallowed up in the gross senses, they become totally unfit for divine contemplations and deep speculations in Nature; their intellectual faculty being drowned in obscurity and dulness, by reason of their sloth, intemperance, or sensual appetites. The followers of Pythagoras enjoined silence, and forbade the eating of the flesh of animals; the first, because they were cautious, and aware of the vanity of vain babbling and fruitless cavillations: they studied the power of numbers to the highest extent; they forbade the eating of flesh not so much on the score of transmigration, as to keep the body in a healthful and temperate state, free from gross humours; by these means they qualified themselves for spiritual matters, and attained unto great and excellent mysteries, and continued in the exercise of charitable arts, and the practice of all moral virtues: yet, seeing they were heathens, they attained not unto the high and inspired lights of wisdom and knowledge that were bestowed on the Apostles, and others, after the coming of Christ; but they mortified their lusts, lived temperately, chaste, honest, and virtuous; which government is so contrary to the practice of modern Christians, that they live as if the blessed word had come upon the earth to grant them privilege to sin. However, we will leave Pythagoras and his followers, to hasten to our own work; whereof we will first explain the foundation of Natural Magic, in as clear and intelligible a manner as the same can be done.

THE

FIRST PRINCIPLES
of
NATURAL MAGIC.

BOOK THE FIRST.

CHAP. I.

NATURAL MAGIC DEFINED---OF MAN----HIS CREATION----DIVINE IMAGE----AND OF THE SPIRITUAL AND MAGICAL VIRTUE OF THE SOUL.

Natural Magic is, as we have said, a comprehensive knowledge of all Nature, by which we search out her secret and occult operations throughout her vast and spacious elaboratory; whereby we come to a knowledge of the component parts, qualities, virtues, and secrets of metals, stones, plants, and animals; but seeing, in the regular order of the creation, man was the work of the sixth day, every thing being prepared for his vicegerency here on earth, and that it pleased the omnipotent God, after he had formed the great world, or macrocosm, and pronounced it good, so he created man the express image of himself; and in man, likewise, an exact model of the great world. We shall describe the wonderful properties of man, in which we may trace in miniature the exact resemblance or copy of the universe; by which means we shall come to the more easy understanding of whatever we may have to declare concerning the knowledge of the inferior nature, such as animals, plants, metals, and stones; for, by our first declaring the occult qualities and properties that are hid in the little world, it will serve as a key to the opening of all the treasures and secrets of the macrocosm, or

great

great world : therefore, we shall hasten to speak of the creation of man, and his divine image; likewise of his fall, in consequence of his disobedience; by which all the train of evils, plagues, diseases, and miseries, were entailed upon his posterity, through the curse of our Creator, but deprecated by the mediation of our blessed Lord, Christ.

THE CREATION, DISOBEDIENCE, AND FALL OF MAN.

ACCORDING to the word of God, which we take in all things for our guide, in the 1st chapter of Genesis, and the 26th verse, it is said—" God said, let us make man in our image, after our likeness; and let them have dominion over the fish of the sea, and over the fowl of the air, and over the cattle, and over *all* the earth, and over every creeping thing that creepeth upon the earth."—Here is the origin and beginning of our frail human nature; hence every soul was created by the very light itself, and Fountain of Life, after his own express image, likewise immortal, in a beautiful and well-formed body, endued with a most excellent mind, and dominion or unlimited monarchy over all Nature, every thing being subjected to his rule, or command; one creature only being excepted, which was to remain untouched and consecrated, as it were, to the divine mandate : "Of every tree of the garden thou mayest freely eat;" "But of the tree of the knowledge of good and evil, thou shalt not eat of it; for in the day that thou eatest of it, thou shalt surely die." Gen. ii. ver. 16.   Therefore Adam was formed by the finger of God, which is the Holy Spirit; whose figure or outward form was beautiful and proportionate as an angel; in whose voice (before he sinned) every sound was the sweetness of harmony and music : had he remained in the state of innocency in which he was formed, the weakness of mortal man, in his depraved state, would not have been able to bear the virtue and celestial shrillness of his voice.   But when the *deceiver* found that man, from the inspiration of God, had began to sing so shrilly, and to repeat the celestial harmony of the heavenly country, he counterfeited the engines of craft : seeing his wrath

against

against him was in vain, he was much tormented thereby, and began to think how he might entangle him into disobedience of the command of his Creator, whereby he might, as it were, laugh him to scorn, in derision of his new creature, man.

Van Helmont, in his Oriatrike, chap. xcii., speaking of the entrance of death into human nature, &c., finely touches the subject of the creation, and man's disobedience : indeed, his ideas so perfectly coincide with my own, that I have thought fit here to transcribe his philosophy, which so clearly explains the text of Scripture, with so much of the light of truth on his side, that it carries along with it the surest and most positive conviction.

" Man being essentially created after the image of God, after that, he rashly presumed to generate the image of God out of himself ; not, indeed, by a certain monster, but by something which was shadowly like himself. With the ravishment of Eve, he, indeed, generated not the image God like unto that which God would have inimitable, as being divine ; but in the vital air of the seed he generated dispositions ; careful at some time to receive a sensitive, discursive, and motive soul from the Father of Light, yet *mortal*, and *to perish ;* yet, nevertheless, he ordinarily inspires, and of his own goodness, the substantial spirit of a mind showing forth his own image : so that man, in this respect, endeavoured to generate his own image ; not after the manner of brute beasts, but by the copulation of seeds, which at length should obtain, by request, a soulified light from the Creator ; and the which they call a sensitive soul.

" For, from thence hath proceeded another generation, conceived after a beast-like manner, mortal, and uncapable of eternal life, after the manner of beasts ; and bringing forth with pains, and subject to diseases, and death ; and so much the more sorrowful, and full of misery, by how much that very propagation in our first parents dared to invert the intent of God.

" Therefore the unutterable goodness forewarned them that they should not taste of that tree ; and otherwise he foretold, that the same day they should die the death, and should feel all the root of calamities which accompanies death."

Deservedly, therefore, hath the Lord deprived both our parents of the benefit of immortality ; namely, death succeeded from a conjugal and brutal copulation ;

neither

neither remained the spirit of the Lord with man, after that he began to be flesh.

Further; because that defilement of Eve shall thenceforth be continued in the propagation of posterity, even unto the end of the world, from hence the sin of the despised fatherly admonition, and natural deviation from the right way, is now among other sins for an impurity, from an inverted, carnal, and well nigh brutish generation, and is truly called original sin; that is, man being sowed in the pleasure of the concupiscence of the flesh, shall therefore always reap a necessary death in the flesh of sin; but, the knowledge of good and evil, which God placed in the dissuaded apple, did contain in it a seminary virtue of the concupiscence of the flesh, that is, an occult forbidden conjunction, diametrically opposite to the state of innocence, which state was not a state of stupidity; because He was he unto whom, before the corruption of Nature, the essences of all living creatures whatsoever were made known, according to which they were to be named from their property, and at their first sight to be essentially distinguished : *man*, therefore, through eating of the apple, attained a knowledge that he had lost his radical innocency; for, neither before the eating of the apple was he so dull or stupified that he knew not, or did not perceive himself naked ; but, with the effect of shame and brutal concupiscence, he then first declared he was naked.

For that the knowledge of good and evil signifies nothing but the concupiscence of the flesh, the Apostle testifies ; calling it the law, and desire of sin. For it pleased the Lord of heaven and earth to insert in the apple an incentive to concupiscence ; by which he was able safely to abstain, by not eating of the apple, therefore dissuaded therefrom ; for otherwise he had never at any time been tempted, or stirred up by his genital members. Therefore the apple being eaten, man, from an occult and natural property ingrafted in the fruit, conceived a lust, and sin became luxurious to him, and from thence was made an animal seed, which, hastening into the previous or foregoing dispositions of a *sensitive soul*, and undergoing the law of other *causes*, reflected itself into the vital spirit of Adam ; and, like an ignis-fatuus, presently receiving an archeus

or

or ruling spirit, and animal idea, it presently conceived a power of propagating an animal and mortal seed, ending into life.

Furthermore, the sacred text hath in many places compelled me unto a perfect position, it making Eve an helper like unto Adam ; not, indeed, that she should supply the *name*, and *room of a wife*, even as she is called, straightway after sin, for she was a virgin in the intent of the Creator, and afterwards filled with misery : but not, as long as the state of purity presided over innocency, did the will of man overcome her ; for the translation of man into Paradise did foreshew another condition of living than that of a beast ; and therefore the eating of the apple doth by a most chaste name cover the concupiscence of the *flesh*, while it contains the " knowledge of good and evil " in this name, and calls the ignorance thereof the state of innocence : for, surely, the attainment of that aforesaid knowledge did nourish a most hurtful death, and an irrevocable deprivation of eternal life : for if man had not tasted the apple, he had lived void of concupiscence, and offsprings had appeared out of Eve (a virgin) from the Holy Spirit.

But the apple being eaten, "presently their eyes were opened," and Adam began lustfully to covet copulation with the naked virgin, and defiled her, the which God had appointed for a naked help unto him. But man prevented the intention of God by a strange generation in the flesh of sin ; whereupon there followed the corruption of the former nature, or the flesh of sin, accompanied by concupiscence : neither doth the text insinuate any other mark of " *the knowledge of good and evil*," than that they " *knew themselves to be naked*," or, speaking properly, of their virginity being corrupted, polluted with bestial lust, and defiled. Indeed, their whole " knowledge of good and evil " is included in their shame within their privy parts alone ; and therefore in the 8th of Leviticus, and many places else in the Holy Scriptures, the privy parts themselves are called by no other etymology than that of shame ; for from the copulation of the flesh their eyes were opened, because they then knew that the good being lost, had brought on them a degenerate nature, shamefulness, an intestine and inevitable obligation of death ; sent also into their posterity.

BOOK I. Alas !

Alas ! too late, indeed they understood, by the unwonted novelty and shamefulness of their concupiscence, why God had so lovingly forbade the eating of the apple. Indeed, the truth being agreeable unto itself, doth attest the filthiness of impure Adamical generation ; for the impurity which had received a contagion from any natural issues whatsoever of menstrues or seed, and that by its touching alone is reckoned equal to that which should by degrees creep on a person from a co-touching of dead carcases, and to be expiated by the same ceremonious rite that the text might agreeably denote, that death began by the concupiscence of the flesh lying hid in the fruit forbidden ; therefore, also, the one only healing medicine, of so great an impurity contracted by touching, consisted in washing : under the similitude or likeness thereof, faith and hope, which in baptism are poured on us, are strengthened.

For as soon as Adam knew that by fratricide the first born of mortals, whom he had begotten in the concupiscence of the flesh, had killed his brother, guiltless and righteous as he was ; and foreseeing the wicked errors of mortals that would come from thence, he likewise perceived his own miseries in himself ; certainly knowing that all these calamities had happened unto him from the sin of concupiscence drawn from the apple, which were unavoidably issuing on his posterity, he thought within himself that the most discreet thing he could do, was hereafter wholly to abstain from his wife, whom he had violated ; and therefore he mourned, in chastity and sorrow, a full hundred years ; hoping that by the merit of that abstinence, and by an opposition to the concupiscence of the flesh, he should not only appease the wrath of the incensed Deity, but that he should again return into the former splendour and majesty of his primitive *innocence* and *purity*. But the repentance of one age being finished, it is most probable the mystery of Christ's incarnation was revealed unto him ; neither that man ever could hope to return to the bright-ness of his ancient purity by his own strength, and much less that himself could reprieve his posterity from death ; and that, therefore, marriage was well pleasing, and was after the fall indulged unto him by God because he had determined thus to satisfy his justice at the fulness of times, which should,

to

to the glory of his own *name*, and the confusion of Satan, elevate mankind to a more sublime and eminent state of blessedness.

From that time Adam began to know his wife, *viz.* after he was an hundred years old, and to fill the earth, by multiplying according to the blessing once given him, and the law enjoined him—" Be fruitful and multiply."—Yet so, nevertheless, that although matrimony, by reason of the great want of propagation, and otherwise impossible coursary succession of the primitive divine generation, be admitted as a sacrament of the faithful.

If, therefore, both our first parents, after the eating of the apple, were ashamed, they covered only their privy parts; therefore that shame doth presuppose, and accuse of something committed against justice—against the intent of the Creator—and against their own proper nature : by consequence, therefore, that Adamical generation was not of the primitive constitution of their nature, as neither of the original intent of the Creator; therefore, when God foretels that the earth shall bring forth thistles and thorns, and that man shall gain his bread by the sweat of his brow, they were not execrations, but admonitions, that those sort of things should be obvious in the earth : and, because that beasts should bring forth in pain—should plow in sweat—should eat their food with labour and fear, that the earth should likewise bring forth very many things besides the intention of the husbandman; therefore, also, that they ought to be nourished like unto brute beasts, who had begun to generate after the manner of brute beasts.

It is likewise told Eve, after her transgression, that she should bring forth in pain. Therefore, what hath the pain of bringing forth common with the eating of the apple, unless the apple had operated about the concupiscence of the flesh, and by consequence stirred up copulation ; and the Creator had intended to dissuade it, by dehorting from the eating of the apple. For, why are the genital members of women punished with pains at child-birth, if the eye in seeing the apple, the hands in cropping it, and the mouth in eating of it, have offended ? for was it not sufficient to have chastised the life with death, and the health with very many diseases ?—Moreover, why is the womb afflicted,

as

as in brutes, with the manner of bringing forth, if the conception granted to beasts were not forbidden to man?

After their fall, therefore, *their eyes were opened, and they were ashamed*: it denotes and signifies that, from the filthiness of concupiscence, they knew that the copulation of the flesh was forbidden in the most pure innocent chastity of nature, and that they were overspread with shame, when, their eyes being opened, their understandings saw that they had committed filthiness most detestable.

But on the serpent and evil spirit alone was the top and summit of the whole curse, even as the privilege of the woman, and the mysterious prerogative of the blessing upon the earth, *viz.* That the woman's seed should bruise the head of the serpent. So that it is not possible that to *bring forth in pain* should be a curse; for truly with the same voice of the Lord is pronounced the blessing of the woman, and victory over the infernal spirit.

Therefore Adam was created in the possession of immortality. God intended not that man should be an *animal* or *sensitive* creature, nor be born, conceived, or live as an animal; for of truth he was created unto a *living soul*, and that after the true image of God; therefore he as far differed from the nature of an animal, as an immortal being from a mortal, and as a God-like creature from a brute.

I am sorry that our school-men, many of them, wish, by their arguments of noise and pride, to draw man into a total animal nature (nothing more), drawing (by their logic) the essence of a man essentially from an animal nature: because, although man afterwards procured death to himself and posterity, and therefore may seem to be made nearer the nature of animal creatures, yet it stood not in his power to be able to pervert the species of the divine image: even so as neither was the evil spirit, of a spirit, made an animal, although he became nearer unto the nature of an animal, by hatred and brutal vices. Therefore man remained in his own species wherein he was created; for as often as man is called an *animal*, or sensitive living creature, and is in earnest thought to be such, so many times the text is falsified which says, " But the serpent was more crafty than all the living creatures of the earth,

earth, which the Lord God had made;" because he speaks of the natural craft and subtilty of that living and creeping animal. Again, if the position be true, man was not directed into the propagation of *seed* or *flesh*, neither did he aspire unto a sensitive soul; and therefore the sensible soul of Adamical generation is not of a brutal species, because it was raised up by a seed which wanted the original ordination and limitation of any species; and so that, as the *sensitive soul* in man arose, besides the intent of the Creator and Nature; so it is of no brutal species, neither can it subsist, unless it be continually tied to the *mind*, from whence it is supported in its life.

Wherefore, while man is of no brutal species, he cannot be an animal in respect to his mind, and much less in respect to his soul, which is of no species.

Therefore know, that neither evil spirit, nor whole nature also, can, by any means or any way whatever, change the essence given unto man from his Creator, and by his foreknowledge determined that he should remain continually such as he was created, although he, in the mean time, hath clothed himself with strange properties, as natural unto him from the vice of his own will; for as it is an absurdity to reckon man glorified among animals, because he is not without sense or feeling, so to be sensitive does not shew the inseparable essence of an animal.

Seeing, therefore, our first parents had both of them now felt the effect throughout their whole bodies of the eating of the apple, or concupiscence of the flesh in their members in Paradise, it shamed them; because their members, which, before, they could rule at their pleasure, were afterwards moved by a proper incentive to lust.

Therefore, on the same day, not only mortality entered through concupiscence, but it presently after entered into a conceived generation; for which they were, the same day, also driven out of Paradise: hence followed an adulterous, lascivious, beast-like, devilish generation, and plainly incapable of entering into the kingdom of God, diametrically opposite to God's ordination; by which means death, and the threatened punishment, *corruption*, became inseparable to man and his posterity.

Therefore,

Therefore, original sin was effectively bred from the concupiscence of the flesh, but occasioned only by the apple being eaten, and the admonition despised : but the stimulative to concupiscence was placed in the dissuaded tree, and that occult lustful property radically inserted and implanted in it. But when Satan (besides his *hope*, and the deflowering of the virgin, nothing hindering of it) saw that man was not taken out of the way, according to the forewarning (for he knew not that the *Son* of *God* had constituted himself a surety, before the Father, for man) he, indeed, looked at the vile, corrupted, and degenerated nature of man, and saw that a power was withdrawn from him of uniting himself to the God of infinite majesty, and began greatly to rejoice. That joy was of short duration, for, by and by, he likewise knew that marriage was ratified by Heaven—that the divine goodness yet inclined to man—and that Satan's own fallacies and deceits were thus deceived : hence conjecturing that the Son of Cod was to restore every defect of contagion, and, therefore, perhaps, to be incarnated. He then put himself to work how, or in what manner, he should defile the stock that was to be raised up by matrimony with a mortal soul, so that he might render every conception of God in vain : therefore he stirred up not only his fratricides, and notoriously wicked persons, that there might be evil abounding at all times; but he procured that Atheism might arise, and that, together with Heathenism, it might daily increase, whereby indeed, if he could not hinder the co-knitting of the immortal mind with the sensitive soul, he might, at least, by destroying the law of Nature, bring man unto a level with himself under infernal punishment : but his special care and desire was to expunge totally the immortal mind out of the stock of posterity.

Therefore he *(the Devil)* stirs up, to this day, detestable copulations in Atheistical libertines : but he saw from thence, that nothing but brutish or savage monsters proceeded, to be abhorred by the very parents themselves; and that the copulation with women was far more plausible to men; and that by this method the generation of men should constantly continue ; for he endeavoured to prevent the hope of restoring a remnant, that is, to hinder the incarnation of the Son of God ; therefore he attempted, by an application of

active

active things, to frame the seed of man according to his own accursed desire;
which, when he had found vain and impossible for him to do, he tried again
whether an imp or witch might not be fructified by sodomy; and when this
did not fully answer his intentions every way, and he saw that of an ass and a
horse a mule was bred, which was nearer a-kin to his mother than his father;
likewise that of a coney and dormouse being the father, a true coney was
bred, being distinct from his mother, only having a tail like the dormouse;
he declined these feats, and betook himself to others worthy, indeed, only of the
subtile craft of the *Prince of Darkness*.

Therefore Satan instituted a connexion of the seed of man with the seed
and in the womb of a junior witch, or sorceress, that he might exclude the
dispositions unto an immortal mind from such a new, polished conception : and
afterwards came forth an adulterous and lascivious generation of Faunii,
Satyrs, Gnomes, Nymphs, Sylphs, Driades, Hamodriades, Neriads, Mermaids,
Syrens, Sphynxes, Monsters, &c., using the constellations, and disposing the
seed of man for such like monstrous prodigious generations.

And, seeing the Faunii and Nymphs of the woods were preferred before the
others in beauty, they afterwards generated their offspring amongst themselves,
and at length began wedlocks with men, feigning that, by these copulations,
they should obtain an immortal soul for them and their offspring; but this
happened through the persuasions and delusions of Satan to admit these
monsters to carnal copulation, which the ignorant were easily persuaded to;
and therefore these Nymphs are called Succubii : although Satan afterwards
committed worse, frequently transchanging himself, by assuming the persons of
both Incubii and Succubii, in both sexes; but they conceived not a true
young by the males, except the Nymphs alone.   The which, indeed, seeing the
sons of God (that is, men) had now, without distinction, and in many places,
taken to be their wives, God was determined to blot out the whole race begotten
by these infernal and detestable marriages, through a deluge of waters, that the
intent of the evil spirit might be rendered frustrate.

Of which monsters before mentioned, I will here give a striking example
from Helmont : for he says, a merchant of Ægina, a countryman of his,
                                                          sailing

sailing various times unto the Canaries, was asked by Helmont for his serious judgment about certain creatures, which the mariners frequently brought home from the mountains, as often as they went, and called them Tude-squils;* for they were dried dead carcasses, almost three-footed, and so small that a boy might easily carry one of them upon the palm of his hand, and they were of an exact human shape; but their whole dead carcass was clear or transparent as any parchment, and their bones flexible like gristles; against the sun, also, their bowels and intestine were plainly to be seen; which thing I, by Spaniards there born, knew to be true. I considered that, to this day, the destroyed race of the Pygmies were there; for the Almighty would render the expectations of the evil spirit, supported by the abominable actions of mankind, void and vain; and he has, therefore, manifoldly saved us from the craft and subtilty of the Devil, unto whom eternal punishments are due, to his extreme and perpetual confusion, unto the everlasting sanctifying of the Divine Name.

CHAP. II.

OF THE WONDERS OF NATURAL MAGIC, DISPLAYED IN A VARIETY OF SYMPATHETIC AND OCCULT OPERATIONS THROUGHOUT THE FAMILIES OF ANIMALS, PLANTS, METALS, AND STONES, TREATED OF MISCELLANEOUSLY.

THE wonders of Animal Magic we mean fully to display under the title of Magnetism. But here we hasten to investigate by what means, instruments, and effects, we must apply actives to passives, to the producing of rare and uncommon effects; whether by *actions, amulets, alligations* and *suspensions* —or *rings, papers, unctions, suffumigations, allurements, sorceries, enchantments, images, lights, sounds,* or the like. Therefore, to begin with things more simple :—If any one shall, with an entire new knife, cut asunder a lemon, using words expressive of hatred, contumely, or dislike, against any individual,

* Stude-quills, or Stew'd quills.

the

the absent party, though at an unlimited distance, feels a certain inexpressible and cutting anguish of the heart, together with a cold chilliness and failure throughout the body ;—likewise of living animals, if a live pigeon be cut through the heart, it causes the heart of the party intended to affect with a sudden failure ; likewise fear is induced by suspending the magical image of a man by a single thread ;—also, death and destruction by means similar to these ; and all these from a fatal and magical sympathy.

Likewise of the virtues of simple animals, as well as manual operations, of which we shall speak more anon :—The application of hare's fat pulls out a thorn ;—likewise any one may cure the tooth-ache with the stone that is in the head of the toad ; also, if any one shall catch a living frog before sun-rise, and he or she spits in the mouth of the frog, will be cured of an asthmatic consumption ;—likewise the right or left eye of the same animal cures blindness ; and the fat of a viper cures a bite of the same. Black hellebore easeth the head-ache, being applied to the head, or the powder snuffed up the nose in a moderate quantity. Coral is a well-known preservative against witchcraft and poisons, which if worn now, in this time, as much round children's necks as usual, would enable them to combat many diseases which their tender years are subjected to, and to which, with fascinations, they often fall a victim. I know how to compose coral amulets, or talismans, which, if suspended even by a thread, shall (God assisting) prevent all harms and accidents of violence from fire, or water, or witchcraft, and help them to withstand all their diseases.

Paracelsus and Helmont both agree, that in the toad, although so irreverent to the sight of man, and so noxious to the touch, and of such strong violent antipathy to the blood of man, I say, out of this hatred Divine Providence hath prepared us a remedy against manifold diseases most inimical to man's nature. The toad hath a natural aversion to man ; and this sealed image, or idea of hatred, he carries in his head, eyes, and most powerfully throughout his whole body : now that the toad may be highly prepared for a sympathetic remedy against the plague or other disorders, such as the ague, falling sicknesses, and various others ; and that the terror of us, and natural inbred hatred may the more strongly be imprinted and higher ascend in the toad, we must hang him up aloft in a chimney, by the legs, and set under him a dish of yellow wax, to receive whatsoever may come down, or fall from his mouth; let him hang in this position, in our sight, for three or four days, at least till he is dead; now we must not omit frequently to be present in sight of the animal, so that his fears and inbred terror of us, with the ideas of strong hatred, may encrease even unto death.

So you have a most powerful remedy in this one toad, for the curing of forty thousand persons infected with the pest or plague.

Van Helmont's process for making a preservative amulet against the plague is as follows :—

"In the month of July, in the decrease of the moon, I took old toads, whose eyes abounded with white worms hanging forth into black heads, so that both his eyes were totally formed with worms, perhaps fifty in number, thickly compacted together, their heads hanging out; and as oft as any one of them attempted to get out, the toad, by applying his fore-foot, forbade its utterance. These toads being hung up, and made to vomit in the manner before mentioned, I reduced the insects and other matters ejected from the toad, with the waxen dish being added thereto; and the dried carcass of the toad being reduced into powder I formed the whole into troches, with gum-dragon; which, being borne about the left breast, drove speedily away all contagion; and being fast bound to the place affected, thoroughly drew out the poison: and these troches were more potent after they had returned into use divers times than when new. I found them to be a most powerful amulet against the plague; for if the serpent eateth dust all the days of his life, because he was the instrument of sinning; so the toad eats earth, (which he vomits up) all the days of his life; and, according to the Adeptical philosophy, the toad bears an hatred to man, so that he infects some herbs that are useful to man with his poison, in order for his death. But this difference note between the toad and the serpent: the toad, at the sight of man, from a natural quality sealed in him, called antipathy, conceives a great terror or astonishment; which terror from man imprints on this animal a natural efficacy against the images of the affrighted archeus in man For, truly the terror of the toad kills and annihilates

hilates the ideas of the affrighted archeus in man, because the terror in the toad is natural, therefore radical."

For the poison of the plague is subdued by the poison of the toad, not by an action primarily destructive, but by a secondary action ; as the pestilent idea of hatred or terror extinguishes the ferment, by whose mediation the poison of the plague subsists, and proceeds to infect : for seeing the poison of the plague is the product of the image of the terrified archeus established in a fermental, putrified odour, and mumial air, this coupling ferments the appropriate mean, and immediately the subject of the poison is taken away.

Therefore the opposition of the amulet formed from the body, &c., of the toad, takes away and prevents the baneful and most horrible effects of the pestilential poison and ferment of the plague.

Hence it is conjectured that he is an animal ordained by God, that the idea of his terror being poisonous indeed to himself, should be to us, and to our plague, a poison in terror. Since, therefore, the toad is most fearful at the beholding of man, which in himself, notwithstanding, forms the terror conceived from man, and also the hatred against man, into an image and active real being, and not consisting only in a confused apprehension ; hence it happens that a poison ariseth in the toad, which kills the pestilent poison of terror in man ; to wit, from whence the archeus waxeth strong, he not only perceiving the pestilent idea to be extinguished in himself ; but, moreover, because he knoweth that something inferior to himself is terrified, dismayed, and doth fly. Again, so great is the fear of the toad, that if he is placed directly before thee, and thou dost behold with an intentive furious look, so that he cannot avoid thee, for a quarter of an hour, he dies,* being fascinated with terror and astonishment.

---

* I have tried this experiment upon the toad, and other reptiles of his nature, and was satisfied of the truth of this affirmation.

OF

OF THE SERPENT.

HIPPOCRATES, by the use of some parts of this animal, attained to himself divine honours; for therewith he cured pestilence and contagion, consumptions, and very many other diseases; for he cleansed the flesh of a viper. The utmost part of the tail and head being cut off, he stripped off the skin, casting away the bowels and gall; he reserved of the intestines only the heart and liver; he drew out all the blood, with the vein running down the back-bone; he bruised the flesh and the aforesaid bowels with the bones, and dried them in a warm oven until they could be powdered, which powder he sprinkled on honey; being clarified and boiled, until he knew that the fleshes in boiling had cast aside their virtue, as well in the broth as in the vapours; he then added unto this electuary the spices of his country to cloak the secret. But this cure of diseases by the serpent contains a great mystery, viz. that as death crept in by the serpent of old, itself ought to be mitigated by the death of the serpent; for Adam, being skilful in the properties of all beasts, was not ignorant also that the serpent was more crafty than other living creatures, and that the aforesaid balsam, the remedy of death, lay hid in the serpent; wherefore the spirit of darkness could not more falsely deceive our first parents than under the guileful serpent's form; for they foolishly imagined they should escape the death, so sorely threatened by God, by the serpent's aid.

Amber is an amulet :—a piece of red amber worn about one, is a preservative against poisons and the pestilence.

Likewise, a sapphire stone is as effectual. Oil of amber, or amber dissolved in pure spirit of wine, comforts the womb being disordered : if a suffumigation of it be made with the warts of the shank of a horse, it will cure many disorders of that region.

The liver and gall of an eel, likewise, being gradually dried and reduced to powder, and taken in the quantity of a filbert-nut in a glass of warm wine, causes a speedy and safe delivery to women in labour. The liver of a serpent likewise effects the same.

Rhubarb,

Rhubarb, on account of its violent antipathy to choler, wonderfully purges the same. Music is a well-known specific for curing the bite of a tarantula, or any venomous spider; likewise, water cures the hydrophobia. Warts are cured by paring off the same; or by burying as many pebbles, secretly, as the party has warts. The king's-evil may be cured by the heart of a toad worn about the neck, first being dried.—Hippomanes excites lust by the bare touch, or being suspended on the party. If any one shall spit in the hand with which he struck, or hurt, another, so shall the wound be cured;—likewise, if any one shall draw the halter wherewith a malefactor was slain across the throat of one who hath the quinsey, it certainly cures him in three days; also, the herb cinque-foil being gathered before sun-rise, one leaf thereof cures the ague of one day; three leaves, cures the tertian; and four, the quartan ague. Rape seeds, sown with cursings and imprecations, grows the fairer, and thrives; but if with praises, the reverse. The juice of deadly nightshade, distilled, and given in a proportionate quantity, makes the party imagine almost whatever you chuse. The herb nip, being heated in the hand, and afterwards you hold in your hand the hand of any other party, they shall never quit you, so long as you retain that herb. The herbs arsemart, comfrey, flaxweed, dragon-wort, adder's-tongue, being steeped in cold water, and if for some time being applied on a wound, or ulcer, they grow warm, and are buried in a muddy place, cureth the wound, or sore, to which they were applied. Again, if any one pluck the leaves of asarabacca, drawing them upwards, they will purge another, who is ignorant of the drawing, by vomit only; but if they are wrested downward to the earth, they purge by stool. A sapphire, or a stone that is of a deep blue colour, if it be rubbed on a tumour, wherein the plague discovers itself, (before the party is too far gone) and by and by it be removed from the sick, the absent jewel attracts all the poison or contagion therefrom. And thus much is sufficient to be said concerning natural occult virtues, whereof we speak in a mixed and miscellaneous manner coming to more distinct heads anon.

CHAP.

CHAP. III.

OF AMULETS, CHARMS, AND ENCHANTMENTS.

THE instrument of enchanters is a pure, living, breathing spirit of the blood, whereby we bind, or attract, those things which we desire or delight in; so that, by an earnest intention of the mind, we take possession of the faculties in a no less potent manner than strong wines beguile the reason and senses of those who drink them; therefore, to charm, is either to bind with words, in which there is great virtue, as the poet sings----

> " Words thrice she spake, which caus'd, at will, sweet sleep ;
> " Appeas'd the troubled waves, and roaring deep."

Indeed, the virtue of man's words are so great, that, when pronounced with a fervent constancy of the mind, they are able to subvert Nature, to cause earthquakes, storms, and tempests. I have, in the country, by only speaking a few words, and used some other things, caused terrible rains and claps of thunder. Almost all charms are impotent without words, because words are the speech of the speaker, and the image of the thing signified or spoken of; therefore, whatever wonderful effect is intended, let the same be performed with the addition of words significative of the *will or desire* of the operator; for words are a kind of occult vehicle of the image conceived or begotten, and sent out of the body by the soul; therefore, all the forcible power of the spirit ought to be breathed out with vehemency, and an arduous and intent desire; and I know how to speak, and convey words together, so as they may be carried onward to the hearer at a vast distance, no other body intervening, which thing I have done often. Words are also oftentimes delivered to us, seemingly by others, in our sleep, whereby we seem to talk and converse; but then no vocal conversations are of any effect, except they proceed from spiritual and occult causes : such spirits have often manifested singular things to me, while in sleep, the which, in waking, I have thought nought of, until conviction of the truth taught me credulity in such like matters.

In

In the late change of Administration, I knew, at least five days before it actually terminated, that it would be as I described to a few of my friends. These things are not alike manifested to every one; only, I believe, to those who have long seriously attended to contemplations of this abstruse nature; but there are those who will say it is not so, merely because they themselves cannot comprehend such things.

However, not to lose time, we proceed. There are various enchantments, which I have proved, relative to common occurrences of life, viz. a kind of binding to that effect which we desire: as to love, or hatred; or to those things we love, or against those things we hate, in all which there is a magical sympathy above the power of reasoning; therefore, those abstruse matters we feel, are convinced of, and reflect upon, and draw them into our use. I will here set down, while speaking of these things, a very powerful amulet for the stopping, immediately, a bloody-flux; for the which (with a faith) I dare lay down my life for the success, and entire cure.

An Amulet for Flux of Blood.

" In the blood of Adam arose death---in the blood of Christ death is ex-
" tinguished---in the same blood of Christ I command thee, O, blood, that
" thou stop fluxing!"*

In this one godly superstition there will be found a *ready*, cheap, easy remedy for that dreadful disorder the bloody-flux, whereby a poor miserable wretch will reap more real benefit than in a whole shop of an apothecary's drugs. These four letters יהוה are a powerful charm, or amulet, against the common ague; likewise, let them be written upon a piece of clean and new vellum, at any time of the day or night, and they will be found a speedy and certain cure, and much more efficacious than the word *Abracadabra:* however, as that ancient charm is still (amongst some who pretend to cure agues, &c.) in some repute, I will here set down the form and manner of its being

---

* Let the party who pronounces these words hold the other's hand.

written

written ;* likewise it must be pronounced, or spoken, in the same order as it is written, with the intent or will of the operator declared at the same time of making it.

CHAP. IV.

OF UNCTIONS, PHILTERS, POTIONS, &c.----THEIR MAGICAL VIRTUES.

UNGUENTS, or unctions, collyries, philters, &c., conveying the virtues of things natural to our spirits, do multiply, transform, transfigure, and transmute it accordingly ; they also transpose *those* virtues, which are in *them*, into *it*, so that it not only acts upon its *own body*, but also upon *that* which is *near it*, and affects that (by visible rays, charms, and by touching it) with some agreeable quality like to itself. For, because our spirit is the *pure, subtil, lucid, airy*, and unctuous vapour of the blood, nothing, therefore, is better adapted for collyriums than the like *vapour*, which are more suitable to our spirit in substance; for then, by reason of their likeness, they do more stir up, attract, and transform the spirit. The same virtue have other ointments, and confections. Hence, by the touch, often plague, sickness, faintings, poisoning, and love, is induced, either by the hands or clothes being anointed; and often by kissing, things been held in the mouth, love is likewise excited.

---

* It is here to be particularly noticed by us, that, in forming of a charm, or amulet, it will be of no effect except the very soul of the operator is strongly and intensely exerted and impressed, as it were, and the image of the idea sealed on the charm, or amulet ; for, without this, in vain will be all the observation of times, hours, and constellations ; therefore, this I have thought fit to mention, once for all, that it may be almost always uppermost in the mind of the operator, for, without this one thing being observed and noticed, many who form seals, &c., do fall short of the wished-for effect.

```
ABRACADABRA
 BRACADABRA
  RACADABRA
   ACADABRA
    CADABRA
     ADABRA
      DABRA
       ABRA
        BRA
         RA
          A
```

Now

Now the sight, as it perceives more purely and clearer than the other senses, seals in *us* the marks of things more acutely, and does, most of all, and before all others, agree with our fantastic spirit ; as is apparent in dreams, when things seen do more often present themselves to us than things heard, or any thing coming under the other senses. Therefore, when collyriums transform the visual spirits, that spirit easily affects the imagination, which, being affected with divers species and forms, transmits the same, by the same spirit, unto the outward sense of sight, by which there is formed in it a perception of such species and forms, in that manner, as if it were moved by external objects, that there appear to be seen terrible images, spirits, and the like. There are some *collyriums* which make us see the *images of spirits in the air*, or elsewhere ; which I can make of the *gall of a man*, and the *eyes of a black cat*, and some other things. The same is made, likewise, of the blood of a lapwing, bat, and a goat ; and if a smooth shining piece of steel be smeared over with the juice of mugwort, and be made to fume, it causes invocated spirits to appear. There are some perfumes, or suffumigations and unctions, which make men speak in their sleep, walk, and do those things that are done by men that are awake, and often what, when awake, they cannot, or dare not do ; others, again, make men hear horrid or delightful sounds, noises, and the like.

And, in some measure, this is the cause why *mad* and melancholy men believe they hear and see things equally false and improbable, falling into most gross and pitiful delusions, fearing where no fear is, and angry where there is none to contend. Such passions as these *we* can induce by *magical vapours, confections, perfumes, collyries, unguents, potions, poisons, lamps, lights,* &c. ; likewise by *mirrors, images, enchantments, charms, sounds,* and *music ;* also by *divers rites, observations, ceremonies, religion,* &c.

CHAP. V.

OF MAGICAL SUSPENSIONS AND ALLIGATIONS——SHEWING HOW, AND BY WHAT POWER, THEY RECEIVE VIRTUE, AND ARE EFFICACIOUS IN NATURAL MAGIC.

WHEN the soul of the world, by its virtue, doth make all things (that are naturally generated, or artificially made) fruitful, by sealing and impressing on them celestial virtues for the working of some wonderful effect, then things themselves not only applied by collyry, or suffume, or ointment, or any other such like way; but when they are conveniently bound to, or wrapped up, or suspended about the neck, or any other way applied, although by ever so easy a contact, they do impress their virtue upon us: by these alligations, &c., therefore, the accidents of the body and mind are changed into sickness or health, valour, fear, sadness or joy, and the like; they render those that carry them, gracious, terrible, acceptable, rejected, honoured, beloved, or hateful and abominable.

Now these kind of passions are conceived to be infused no otherwise than is manifest in the grafting of trees, where the vital life and virtue is communicated from the trunk to the twig engrafted into it, by way of contact and alligation; so in the female palm-tree, when she comes near to the male, her boughs bend to the male, which the gardener seeing, he binds them together by ropes across, but soon becomes straight, as if by the continuation of the rope she had received a propagating virtue from the male. And it is said, if a woman takes a needle, and bewray it with dung, and put it up in earth in which the carcass of a man has been buried, and carry it about her in a piece of cloth used at a funeral, no man can defile her as long as she carries that.

Now by these examples we see how, by certain alligations of certain things, also suspensions, or by the most simple contact or continuation of any thread, we may be able to receive some virtues thereby; but it is necessary to know the certain rule of magical alligation and suspension; and the manner that the art requires is this, viz. that they must be done under a certain and suitable constellation; and they must be done with wire, or silken threads, or sinews

of

of certain animals; and those things that are to be wrapped up, are to be done in the leaves of herbs, or skins of animals, or membraneous parchments, &c. For, if you would procure the *solary* virtue of any thing, this is to be wrapped up in bay leaves, or the skin of a lion, hung round the neck with gold, silk, or purple or yellow thread: while the sun reigns in the heavens, so shalt thou be endued with the virtue of that thing. So if a saturnine quality or thing be desired, thou shalt in like manner take that thing, while Saturn reigns, and wrap it up in the skin of an ass, or in a cloth used at a funeral, especially if melancholy or sadness is to be induced, and with a sad, or ash, or leaden, or black silk or thread, hang it about thy neck; and so in the same manner we must proceed with the rest.

CHAP. VI.

OF ANTIPATHIES.

IT is necessary, in this place, to speak of the *antipathies of natural things*, seeing it is requisite, as we go on, to have a thorough knowledge of that obstinate contrariety of Nature, where any thing shuns its contrary, and drives it, as it were, out of its presence. Such antipathy as this has the root rhubarb against choler; treacle against poison; the *sapphire stone against hot biles*, feverish heats, and diseases of the eyes; the *amethyst* against drunkenness; the *jasper* against the bloody-flux and offensive imaginations; the *emerald*, and *agnus castus* against lust; *achates or agates* against poison; piony against the falling sickness; *coral* against the ebullition of black choler, and pains of the stomach; the *topaz* against spiritual heats, such as are covetousness, lust, and all manner of love excesses. The same antipathy is there, also, of pismires against the herb organ, and the wing of a bat, and the heart of a lapwing, from the presence of which they fly. Also, the organ is contrary to a certain poisonous fly which cannot resist the sun, and resists salamanders, and loaths cabbage with such a deadly hatred that they cannot endure each other.

So

So they say cucumbers hate oil. And the gall of a crow makes even men fearful, and drives them from the place wherein it is placed. *A diamond* disagrees with a *loadstone*; that being present, it suffers no iron to be drawn to it. Sheep avoid frog-parsley as a deadly thing ; and, what is more wonderful, Nature hath depictured the sign of this antipathy upon the livers of sheep, in which the very figure of frog-parsley doth naturally appear. Again, goats hate garden-basil, as if there was nothing more pernicious. And, amongst animals, mice and weasels disagree ; so a lizard is of a contrary nature to a scorpion, and induces great terror to the scorpion with its very sight, and they are therefore killed with the oil of them ; which oil will likewise cure the wounds made by scorpions. There is a great enmity between scorpions and mice ; therefore if a mouse be applied to the bite of a scorpion, he cures it. Nothing is so much an enemy to snakes as crabs ; and if swine be hurt by them, they are cured by crabs ; the sun, also being in Cancer, serpents are tormented. Also, the scorpion and crocodile kill one another ; and if the bird ibis does but touch a crocodile with one of his feathers, he makes him unmoveable. The bird called a bustard flies away at the sight of a horse ; and a hart at the sight of a ram, or a viper. An elephant trembles at the hearing of the grunting of a hog ; so doth a lion at the crowing of a cock ; and a panther will not touch them that are anointed with the fat of a hen, especially if garlick has been put into it. There is also an enmity between foxes and swans ; bulls and jackdaws. And some birds are at a perpetual variance, as daws and owls ; kites and crows ; turtle and ring-tail ; egepis and eagles ; also, harts and dragons. Amongst water animals, there is a great antipathy between dolphins and whirlpools ; the mullet and pike ; lamprey and conger ; pourcontrel and lobster, which latter, but seeing the former, is nearly struck dead with fear ; but the lobster tears the conger. The civet-cat cannot resist the panther ; and if the skins of both be hung up against each other, the skin or hairs of the panther will fall off. Apollo says, in his hieroglyphics, if any one be girt about with the skin of a civet-cat, he may pass safe through his enemies. The lamb flies from the wolf ; and if the tail, skin, or head of lupus be hung up in the sheeps'-cot, they cannot eat their meat for very fear.

And

And Pliny mentions the bird called the marlin, that breaks the eggs of the crow, whose young are annoyed by the fox; that she also will pinch the whelps of the fox, and the fox likewise, which, when the crow sees, they help the fox against her as against a common enemy. The linnet lives in, and eats thistles; yet she hates the ass, because he eats the thistles and flowers of them. There is so great an enmity between the little bird called esalon and the ass, that their blood will not mix; and that, at the simple braying of the ass, both the esalon's eggs and young perish together. There is, also, a total antipathy of the olive-tree to the harlot; that, if she plant it, it will neither thrive nor prosper, but wither. A lion fears lighted torches, and is tamed by nothing sooner. The wolf fears not sword or spear, but a stone; by the throwing of which a wound being made, worms breed in the wolf. A horse fears a camel so much that he cannot endure the picture of that beast. An elephant, when he rages, is quieted by seeing a cock. A snake is afraid of a naked man, but pursues one clothed. A mad bull is tamed by being tied to a fig-tree. Amber attracts all things to it but garden-basil, and things smeared with oil, between which there is a natural antipathy.

CHAP. VII.

OF THE OCCULT VIRTUES OF THINGS WHICH ARE INHERENT IN THEM ONLY IN THEIR LIFE-TIME, AND SUCH AS REMAIN IN THEM EVEN AFTER DEATH.

IT is expedient for us to know that there are some things which retain virtue only while they are living, others even after death. So in the cholic, if a live duck be applied to the belly, it takes away the pain, and the duck dies. If you take the heart out of any animal, and, while it is warm, bind it to one that has a quartan fever, it drives it away. So if any one shall swallow the heart of a lapwing, swallow, weasel, or a mole, while it is yet living and warm with natural heat, it improves his intellect, and helps him to remember, understand, and foretel things to come. Hence this general rule,---that what-

ever

ever things are taken for magical uses from animals, whether they are stones, members, hair, excrements, nails, or any thing else, they must be taken from those animals while they are yet alive, and, if it is possible, that they may live afterwards. If you take the tongue of a frog, you put the frog into water again; — and Democritus writes, that if any one shall take out the tongue of a water-frog, no other part of the animal sticking to it, and lay it upon the place where the heart beats of a woman, she is compelled, against her will, to answer whatsoever you shall ask of her. Also, take the eyes of a frog, which must be extracted before sun-rise, and bound to the sick party, and the frog to be let go again blind into the water, the party shall be cured of a tertian ague; also, the same will, being bound with the flesh of a nightingale in the skin of a hart, keep a person always wakeful without sleeping. Also, the roe of the fork fish being bound to the navel, is said to cause women an easy child-birth, if it be taken from it alive, and the fish put into the sea again. So the right eye of a serpent being applied to the soreness of the eyes, cures the same, if the serpent be let go alive. So, likewise, the tooth of a mole, being taken out alive, and afterwards let go, cures the tooth-ache; and dogs will never bark at those who have the tail of a weasel that has escaped. Democritus says, that if the tongue of the cameleon be taken alive, it conduces to good success in trials, and likewise to women in labour; but it must be hung up on some part of the outside of the house, otherwise, if brought into the house, it might be most dangerous.

There are very many properties that remain after death; and these are things in which the idea of the matter is less swallowed up, *according to Plato*, in them: even after death, that which is immortal in them will work some wonderful things :—as in the skins we have mentioned of several wild beasts, which will corrode and eat one another after death; also, a drum made of the rocket-fish drives away all creeping things at what distance soever the sound of it is heard; and the strings of an instrument made of the guts of a wolf, and being strained upon a harp or lute, with strings made of sheep-guts, will make no harmony.

CHAP.

CHAP. VIII.

OF THE WONDERFUL VIRTUES OF SOME KIND OF PRECIOUS STONES.

IT is a common opinion of magicians, that stones inherit great virtues, which they receive through the spheres and activity of the celestial influences, by the medium of the soul or spirit of the world. Authors very much disagree in respect of the probability of their actually having such virtues in potentia, some debating warmly against any occult or secret virtue lying hid in them; others, as warmly, shewing the causes and effects of these sympathetic properties. However, to leave these trifling arguments to those who love cavil and contentions better than I do, and, as I have neither leisure nor inclination to enter the lists with sophists, and tongue-philosophers; I say, that these occult virtues are disposed throughout the animal, vegetable, and mineral kingdoms, by seeds, or ideas originally emanating from the Divine mind, and through supercelestial spirits and intelligence always operating, according to their proper offices and governments allotted them; which virtues are infused, as we before said, through the medium of the Universal Spirit, as by a general and manifest sympathy and antipathy established in the law of Nature. Amongst a variety of examples, the loadstone is one most remarkable proof of the sympathy and antipathy we speak of. However to hasten to the point. Amongst stones, those which resemble the rays of the sun by their golden sparklings, (as does the glittering stone ætites) prevent the falling-sickness and poisons, if worn on the finger; so the stone which is called *oculis solis*, or eye of the sun, being in figure like to the apple of the eye, from which shines forth a ray, comforts the brain, and strengthens sight; the carbuncle, which shines by night, hath a virtue against all airy and vaporous poisons; the chrysolite stone, of a light green colour, when held against the sun, there shines in it a ray like a star of gold; this is singularly good for the lungs, and cures asthmatical complaints; and if it be bored through, and the hollow filled with the mane of an ass, and bound to the left arm, it chases away all foolish and idle imaginations and melancholy fears, and drives away folly.

The

The stone called iris, which is like crystal in colour, being found with six corners, when held in the shade, and the sun suffered to shine through it, represents a natural rainbow in the air. The stone heliotropium, green, like a jasper or emerald, beset with red specks, makes the wearer constant, renowned, and famous, and conduces to long life; there is, likewise, another wonderful property in this stone, and that is, that it so dazzles the eyes of men, that it causes the bearer to be invisible; but then there must be applied to it the herb bearing the same name, viz. heliotropium, or the sun-flower; and these kind of virtues Albertus Magnus, and William of Paris, mention in their writings. The jacinth also possesses virtue from the sun against poisons, pestilences, and pestiferous vapours; likewise it renders the bearer pleasant and acceptable; conduces, also, to gain money; being simply held in the mouth, it wonderfully cheers the heart, and strengthens the mind. Then there is the pyrophilus, of a red mixture, which Albertus Magnus reports that Æsculapius makes mention of in one of his epistles to Octavius Cæsar, saying, " There is a certain poison, so intensely cold, which preserves the heart of man, being taken out, from burning; so that if it be put into the fire for any time, it is turned into a stone, which stone is called *pyrophilus:* " it possesses a wonderful virtue against poison; and it infallibly renders the wearer thereof renowned and dreadful to his enemies. Apollonius is reported to have found a stone called pantaura, (which will attract other stones, as the loadstone does iron) most powerful against all poisons: it is spotted like the panther, and therefore some naturalists have given this stone the name of pantherus: Aaron calls it evanthum; and some, on account of its variety, call it pantochras.

CHAP.

CHAP. IX.

OF THE MIXTURES OF NATURAL THINGS ONE WITH ANOTHER, AND THE PRODUCING OF
MONSTROUS ANIMALS, BY THE APPLICATION OF NATURAL MAGIC.

MAGICIANS, students, and observers of the operations of Nature, know
how, by the application of active forms to a matter fitly disposed, and made,
as it were, a proper recipient, to effect many wonderful and uncommon things
that seem strange, and above Nature, by gathering this and that thing bene-
ficial and conducive to that effect which we desire ; however, it is evident that
all the powers and virtues of the inferior bodies are not found comprehended
in any one single thing, but are dispersed amongst many of the compounds
here amongst us ; wherefore it is necessary, if there be a hundred virtues
of the sun dispersed through so many animals, plants, metals, or stones,
we should gather all these together, and bring them all into one form, in which
we shall see all the said virtues, being united, contained.   Now there is a
double virtue in commixing : one, viz. which was once planted in its parts,
and is *celestial*; the other is obtained by a certain artificial mixture of things,
mixed among themselves, according to a due proportion, such as agree with
the heavens under a certain constellation ; and this virtue descends by a certain
similitude or likeness that is in things amongst themselves, by which they
are drawn or attracted towards their superiors, and as much as the following do
by degrees correspond with them that go before, where the patient is fitly
applied to its agent.   So from a certain composition of *herbs, vapours*, and such
like, made according to the rules of Natural and Celestial Magic, there results
a certain common form ; of which we shall deliver the true and infallible rules
and experiments in our Second Book, where we have written expressly on the
same.

We ought, likewise, to understand that by how much more noble and excellent the form of any thing is, by so much the more it is prone, and apt to
receive, and powerful to act.   Then the virtue of things do indeed become
wonderful ; viz. when they are applied to matters, mixed and prepared in fit

BOOK I.   seasons

seasons to give them life, by procuring life for them from the stars, our own spirit powerfully co-operating therewith; for there is so great a power in prepared matters, which we see do then receive life, when a perfect mixture of qualities do break the former contrariety; for so much the more perfect life things receive, by as much the temper and composition is free from contrariety. Now the heavens, as a prevailing cause, do, from the beginning of every thing, (to be generated by the concoction and perfect digestion of the matter) together with life, bestow celestial influences and wonderful gifts, according to the capacity that is in that life and sensible soul to receive more noble and sublime virtues. For the celestial virtue otherwise lies asleep, as sulphur kept from flame; but in living bodies it doth always burn, as kindled sulphur, which, by its vapour, fills all the places that are near.

There is a book called, "A Book of the Laws of Pluto," which speaks of monstrous generations, which are not produced according to the laws of Nature. Of these things which follow we know to be true; viz. of worms are generated gnats; of a horse, wasps; of a calf and ox, bees. Take a living crab, his legs being broken off, and he buried under the earth, a scorpion is produced. If a duck be dried into powder, and put into water, frogs are soon generated; but if he be baked in a pie, and cut into pieces, and be put in a moist place under ground, toads are generated. Of the herb garden-basil, bruised, and put between two stones, are generated scorpions. Of the hairs of a menstruous woman, put under dung, are bred serpents; and the hair of a horse's tail, put into water, receives life, and is turned into a most pernicious worm. And there is an art wherewith a hen, sitting upon eggs, may be generated the form of a man, which I myself know how to do, and which magicians call the mandrake, and it hath in it wonderful virtues.

You must, therefore, know which and what kind of matters are either of art or nature, begun or perfected, or compounded of more things, and what celestial influences they are able to receive. For a congruity of natural things is sufficient for the receiving of influence from celestial; because, nothing hindering, the celestials send forth their light upon inferiors; they suffer no matter to be destitute of their virtue. Wherefore as much matter as is *perfect* and

pure

pure is, as we before said, fitted to receive celestial influences; for that is the binding and continuing of the matter of the soul to the world, which doth daily flow in upon things natural, and all things which *Nature hath prepared*, that it is impossible that a prepared matter should not receive life, or a more noble form.

CHAP. X.

OF THE ART OF FASCINATION, BINDING, SORCERIES, MAGICAL CONFECTIONS, LIGHTS, CANDLES, LAMPS, &c. &c.; BEING THE CONCLUSION OF THE NATURAL MAGIC.*

WE have so far spoken concerning the great virtues, and wonderful efficacy, of natural things; it remains now that we speak of a wonderful power and faculty of fascination; or, more properly, a magical and occult binding of men into love or hatred, sickness or health;—also, the binding of thieves, that they cannot steal in any place; or to bind them that they cannot remove, from whence they may be detected;—the binding of merchants, that they cannot buy nor sell;—the binding of an army, that they cannot pass over any bounds;—the binding of ships, so that no wind, though ever so strong, shall be able to carry them out of that harbour;—the binding of a mill, that it cannot, by any means whatsoever, be turned to work;—the binding of a cistern, or fountain, that the water cannot be drawn up out of them;—the binding of the ground, so that nothing will bring forth fruit, or flourish in it; also, that nothing can be built upon it;—the binding of fire, that, though it be ever so strong, it shall burn no combustible thing that is put to it;—also, the binding of lightnings and tempests, that they shall do no hurt;—the binding of dogs, that they cannot bark;—also, the binding of birds and wild beasts, that they shall not be able to run or fly away; and things familiar to

---

* The latter part of this Chapter serves as a rule to be observed in the composition of all kinds of mixed experiments; and it is as appropriate to the materials collected for talismans, seals, &c. treated of in our Celestial Magic, Book II.   *F. B.*

these,

these, which are hardly creditable, yet known by experience. Now how it is that these kind of bindings are made and brought to pass, we must know. They are thus done : by sorceries, collyries, unguents, potions, binding to and hanging up of talismans, by charms, incantations, strong imaginations, affections, passions, images, characters, enchantments, imprecations, lights, and by sounds, numbers, words, names, invocations, swearings, conjurations, consecrations, and the like.

OF SORCERIES.

THE force of sorceries are, no doubt, very powerful; indeed, they are able to confound, subvert, consume, and change all inferior things; likewise there are sorceries by which we can suspend the faculties of men and beasts. Now, as we have promised, we will shew what some of these kind of sorceries are, that, by the example of these, there may be a way opened for the whole subject of them. Of these, the first is menstruous blood, which, how much power it has in sorcery, we will now consider :—First, if it comes over new wine, it will turn it sour; and if it does but touch a vine, it will spoil it for ever; and, by its very touch, it renders all plants and trees barren, and those newly set, die; it burns up all the herbs in the garden, and makes fruit fall from trees ; it makes dim the brightness of a looking-glass, dulls the edges of knives and razors, dims the beauty of polished ivory, and makes iron rusty ; it likewise makes brass rusty, and to smell very strong ; by the taste, it makes dogs run mad, and, being thus mad, if they once bite any one, that wound is incurable ; it destroys whole hives of bees, and drives them away, if it does but touch them ; it makes linen black that is boiled with it ; it makes mares cast their foals by touching them with it, and women miscarry ; it makes asses barren if they eat of the corn touched by it. The ashes of menstruous clothes cast upon purple garments, that are to be washed, change their colour, and likewise take away the colour of flowers. It also drives away tertian and quartan agues, if it be put into the wool of a black ram, and tied up in a silver

silver bracelet; as also if the soles of the patient's feet be anointed therewith, and especially if it be done by the woman herself, the patient not knowing what she uses. It likewise cures the falling sickness; but most especially it cures them that are afraid of water or drink after they are bitten by a mad dog, if only a menstruous cloth be put under the cup. Likewise, if a menstruous woman shall walk naked, before sun-rise, in a field of standing corn, all hurtful things perish; but if after sun-rise, the corn withers; also, they are able to expel hail, rain, thunders, and lightnings; more of which Pliny mentions. Know this, that if they happen at the decrease of the moon, they are a much greater poison than in the increase, and yet much greater if they happen between the decrease and change; but if they happen in the eclipse of the sun or moon, they are a most incurable and violent poison. But they are of the greatest force when they happen in the first years of the virginity, for then if they but touch the door-posts of a house, no mischief can take effect in it. And some say that the threads of any garment touched therewith cannot be burnt, and if they are cast into a fire, it will spread no farther. Also it is noted, that the root of piony being given with castor, and smeared over with a menstruous cloth, it certainly cureth the falling sickness.

Again, let the stomach of a hart be roasted, and to it be put a perfume made with a menstruous cloth; it will make cross-bows useless for the killing of any game. The hairs of a menstruous woman, put under dung, breeds serpents; and if they are burnt, will drive away serpents with the fume. So great and powerful a poison is in them, that they are a poison to poisonous creatures.

We next come to speak of hippomanes, which, amongst sorceries, are not accounted the least: and this is a little venemous piece of flesh, the size of a fig, and black, which is in the forehead of a colt newly foaled, which, unless the mare herself doth presently eat, she will hardly ever love her foles, or let them suck; and this is a most powerful philter to cause love, if it be powdered, and drank in a cup with the blood of him that is in love: such a potion was given to Medea by Jason.

There is another sorcery which is called hippomanes, viz. a venomous liquor issuing out of the share of a mare at the time she lusts after the horse. The
civet-

civet-cat, also, abounds with sorceries; for the posts of a door being touched with her blood, the arts of jugglers and sorcerers are so invalid that evil spirits can by no means be called up, or compelled to talk with them :---This is Pliny's report. Also, those that are anointed with the oil of her left foot, being boiled with the ashes of the ancle bone of the same and the blood of a weasel, shall become odious to all. The same, also, is to be done with the eye being decocted. If any one hath a little of the strait-gut of this animal about him, and it is bound to the left arm, it is a charm; that if he does but look upon a woman, it will cause her to follow him at all opportunities; and the skin of this animal's forehead withstands witchcraft.

We next come to speak of the blood of a basilisk, which magicians call the blood of Saturn.---This procures (by its virtue) for him that carries it about him, good success of petitions from great men; likewise makes him amazingly successful in the cure of diseases, and the grant of any privilege. They say, also, that a tike, if it be taken out of the left ear of a dog, and it be altogether black, if the sick person shall answer him that brought it in, and who, standing at his feet, shall ask him concerning his disease, there is certain hope of life; and that he shall die if he make him no answer. They say, also, that a stone bitten by a mad dog causes discord, if it be put into drinks; and if any one shall put the tongue of a dog, dried, into his shoe, or some of the powder, no dog is able to bark at him who hath it; and more powerful this, if the herb hound's-tongue be put with it. And the membrane of the secundine of a bitch does the same; likewise, dogs will not bark at him who hath the heart of a dog in his pocket.

The red toad (Pliny says) living in briers and brambles, is full of sorceries, and is capable of wonderful things : there is a little bone in his left side, which being cast into cold water, makes it presently hot; by which, also, the rage of dogs are restrained, and their love procured, if it be put in their drink, making them faithful and serviceable; if it be bound to a woman, it stirs up lust. On the contrary, the bone which is on the right side makes hot water cold, and it binds it so that no heat can make it hot while it there remains. It is a certain cure for quartans, if it be bound to the sick in a snake's skin; and like-

wise

wise cures all fevers, the St. Anthony's fire, and restrains love and lust. And the spleen and heart are effectual antidotes against the poisons of the said toad. Thus much Pliny writes.

Also it is said, that the sword with which a man is slain hath wonderful power ; for if the snaffle of a bridle, or bit, or spurs, be made of it, with these a horse ever so wild is tamed, and made gentle and obedient. They say, if we dip a sword, with which any one was beheaded, in wine, that it cures the quartan, the sick being given to drink of it. There is a liquor made, by which men are made as raging and furious as a bear, imagining themselves in every respect to be changed into one ; and this is done by dissolving or boiling the brains and heart of that animal in new wine, and giving any one to drink out of a skull, and, while the force of the draught operates, he will fancy every living creature to be a bear like to himself; neither can any thing divert or cure him till the fumes and virtue of the liquor are entirely expended, no other distemper being perceivable in him.

The most certain cure of a violent head-ache, is to take any herb growing upon the top of the head of an image ; the same being bound, or hung about one with a red thread, it will soon allay the violent pain thereof.

OF MAGICAL LIGHTS, CANDLES, LAMPS, &c.

THERE are made, artificially, some kinds of lamps, torches, candles, and the like, of some certain and appropriate materials and liquors opportunely gathered and collected for this purpose, which, when they are lighted and shine alone, produce some wonderful effects. There is a *poison* from mares, after copulation, which, being lighted in torches composed of their fat and marrow, doth represent on the walls a monstrous deformity of horses' heads, which thing is both easy and pleasant to do : the like may be done of asses and flies. And the skin of a serpent or snake, lighted in a green lamp, makes the images of the same to appear ; and grapes produce the same effect, if, when they are

in

in their flowers, you shall take a phial, and bind it to them, filled with oil, and shall let them remain so till they are ripe, and then the oil be lighted in a lamp, you shall see a prodigious quantity of grapes; and the same in other fruits. If centaury be mixed with honey and the blood of a lapwing, and be put in a lamp, they that stand about will be of a gigantic stature; and if it be lighted in a clear evening, the stars will seem scattered about.

The ink of the cuttle-fish being put into a lamp, makes Blackamoors appear. So, also, a candle made of some saturnine things, such as man's fat and marrow, the fat of a black cat, with the brains of a crow or raven, which being extinguished in the mouth of a man lately dead, will afterwards, as often as it shines alone, bring great horror and fear upon the spectators about it.

Of such like *torches*, *candles*, *lamps*, &c., (of which we shall speak further in our Book of *Magnetism and Mummies*) Hermes speaks largely of; also Plato and Chyrannides; and, of the later writers, Albertus Magnus makes particular mention of the truth and efficacy of these, in a treatise on these particular things relative to lights, &c.

OF THE ART OF FASCINATION, OR BINDING BY THE LOOK OR SIGHT.

WE call fascination a binding, because it is effected by a look, glance, or observation, in which we take possession of the spirit, and overpower the same, of those we mean to fascinate or suspend; for it comes through the eyes, and the instrument by which we fascinate or bind is a certain, pure, lucid, subtil spirit, generated out of the ferment of the purer blood by the heat of the heart, and the firm, determined, and ardent will of the soul which directs it to the object previously disposed to be fascinated. This doth always send forth by the eyes rays or beams, carrying with them a pure subtil spirit or vapour into the eye or blood of him or her that is opposite. So the eye, being opened and intent upon any one with a strong imagination, doth dart its beams, which are the

vehicle

vehicle of the spirit, into whatever we will affect or bind, which spirit striking
the eye of them who are fascinated, being stirred up in the heart and soul of
him that sends them forth, and possessing the breast of them who are struck,
wounds their hearts, infects their spirits, and overpowers them.

Know, likewise, that in witches, those are most bewitched, who, with often
looking, direct the edge of their sight to the edge of the sight of those who
bewitch or fascinate them ; whence arose the saying of " Evil eyes, &c."
For when their eyes are reciprocally bent one upon the other, and are joined
beams to beams, and lights to lights, then the spirit of the one is joined to
the spirit of the other, and then are strong ligations made ; and most violent
love is stirred up, only with a sudden looking on, as it were, with the darting
a look, or piercing into the very inmost of the heart, whence the spirit and
amorous blood, being thus wounded, are carried forth upon the lover, and
enchanter ; no otherwise than the spirit and the blood of him that is murdered
is upon the murderer, who, if standing near the body killed, the blood flows
afresh, which thing has been tried by repeated experiments.

So great power is there in fascination that many uncommon and wonderful
things are thereby effected, especially when the vapours of the eyes are sub-
servient to the affection ; therefore collyries, ointments, alligations, &c. are
used to affect and corroborate the spirit in this or that manner : to induce
love, they use venereal collyriums, as hippomanes, blood of doves, &c.   To
induce fear, they use martial collyriums, as the eyes of wolves, bear's fat,
and the civet-cat.   To procure misery, or sickness, they use saturnine, and
so on.

Thus much we have thought proper to speak concerning Natural Magic,
in which we have, as it may be said, only opened the first chamber of Nature's
storehouse ; *indeed we should have inserted many more things here*, but as
they fall more properly under the heads of *Magnetism, Mummy*, &c., to
which we refer the reader, we shall take our leave of the reader for the
present, that we may give him time to breathe, likewise to digest what he has
here feasted upon ; and, while he is preparing to enter the unlocked chambers

of Magic and Nature, we will procure him a rich service of most delicious
meats, fit for the hungry and thirsty traveller through the vast labyrinths of
wisdom and true science.

END OF THE NATURAL MAGIC.

THE Author having, under the title of Natural Magic, collected and
arranged every thing that was curious, scarce, and valuable, as well his own
experiments, as those in which he has been indefatigable in gathering from
the science and practice of Magical Authors, and those the most ancient and
abstruse, as may be seen in the list at the end of the Book, where he has put
down the names of the authors, from which he has translated many things
that were never yet published in the English language, particularly *Hermes,
Tritemius, Paracelsus, Bacon, Dee, Porta, Agrippa,* &c. &c. &c. ; from whom
he has not been ashamed to borrow what he thought and knew would be
valuable and gratifying to the sons of Wisdom, in addition to many other rare
and uncommon experiments relative to this art.

THE

THE

TRUE SECRET OF THE PHILOSOPHERS' STONE;

OR,

JEWEL OF ALCHYMY.

WHEREIN

THE PROCESS OF MAKING THE GREAT ELIXIR

is discovered ;

BY WHICH BASE METALS MAY BE TURNED INTO PURE GOLD; CONTAINING THE MOST
EXCELLENT AND PROFITABLE INSTRUCTIONS IN THE

HERMETIC ART ;

DISCOVERING THAT VALUABLE AND SECRET

MEDICINE OF THE PHILOSOPHERS,

To make Men Healthy, Wise, and Happy.

BY F. BARRETT,

STUDENT OF CHEMISTRY, NATURAL PHILOSOPHY, &c.

1801.

EPISTLE TO MUSEUS.

" Thou, O, Museus ! whose mind is high,
" Observe my words, and read them with thine eye ;
" These secrets in thy sacred breast repone,
" And in thy journey think of God alone ;
" The Author of all things, that cannot die ;
" Of whom we now shall speak———"

I TELL thee here, Museus, to observe our words, and read them with thine eye, that is, the eye of thine understanding; for, know, there are many that hear us speak, that read not the meaning of our words. Wherefore shouldst thou contemplate these mysteries with so much constancy of mind, if thou didst not perceive in them some great good most desirable ?— Listen, then, O, young man, and hear our words ! We will shew thee the dangerous precipice of vanity and head-long desire—we will describe to thee the stubborn and fatal will of our passions, even with tears of contrition, and heart-felt compassion for thy inexperience—we will lead thee, as it were, by the hand, through those labyrinths of vice, wherewith thou art daily surrounded; and, however prejudiced thou mightest be against the receiving of our doctrine, yet, be assured, we have in our possession the magical virtue and power of binding thee to our principles, and making thee happy, in spite of thyself. Here is a great secret ! thou shalt say---every man wishes to be happy—which I grant; but my answer is—most men prevent their own happiness; they destroy it, by suffering themselves to be governed by the outward principle of the flesh, thinking the *greatest good* to be in the satisfying of their carnal appetites, or in the amassing together heaps of wealth, whereby they thrust down the meek and poor, raising up the standards of Pride, Envy, and Oppression. These things every day's experience confirms; nay, there are some so blind, that, in the possession of much wealth, they think there is nothing

beyond

beyond it; insomuch, that they triumph in *lust, oppression, revenge,* and *contumely.* But how is it, thou wilt say, that, seeing man is a reasonable being, he can possibly give up his government so easily?—I say, when man suffers the unreasonable and bestial part to deprave him, then he immediately becomes a slave, (and the vilest of slavery is that which deprives man of his social virtues;) for then, although in the possession of great worldy things, such as houses, estates, and all other temporal gifts, yet he becomes an immediate instrument to the Prince of this World and the Powers of Darkness, seeing that those riches he inherits are merely given him in this life, to bestow upon others those necessaries and comforts which he himself does not feel the want of, and by which he might, if not blinded by his passions and lusts, secure himself an eternal and incorruptible treasure. But he who possesses treasures without mercy, liberality, bounty, charity, &c., robs the Eternal Author of all good, of the honour due unto him, and, in short, is working destruction to his own soul; his riches, instead of benefitting himself and others, eventually and finally terminates as a curse : while he lives here he is a scourge to society; and, after he leaves this, it is plain enough pointed out in the New Testament what will be his situation and condition.

Therefore, thou young man, that hast but a few years to live, study how to attain the stone we teach of : it will protract the beauty of thy youth, though thou shouldst live for centuries—it will ever supply thee with the means of comforting the afflicted; insomuch, that when thou hast attained this truly desirable and most perfect talisman, thy life will become soft and pleasant; no cares, nor corroding pangs—no self-torment will ever invade thy mind; neither shalt thou want the means to be happy, in respect of the possession of the goods of this life, but shalt have abundantly. But how, and from what source, all this is to proceed---out of what *thing* or *matter* thou shalt attain thy wished-for end---the studying of the ensuing Treatise will sufficiently shew.

Thy Friend,

F. B.

TO

TO THE READER.

ALTHOUGH we do not, in any point of science, arrogate perfection in ourselves, yet something we have attained by dear experience, by diligent labour, and by study, worthy of being communicated for the instruction of either the licentious libertine, or the grave student—the observer of Nature; and this, our Work, we concentrated into a *focus:* it is, as it were, a spiritual essence drawn from a large quantity of matter; for we can say, with propriety, that this little Treatise is truly spiritual, and essential to the happiness of man: therefore, to those who wish to be happy, with every good intention we commend this Work to be their constant companion and study, in which, if they persevere, they shall not fail of their desires in the attainment of the true Philosophers' Stone.

PART

PART THE FIRST.

OF ALCHYMY, ITS DIVINE ORIGIN, &c.----DIFFICULTY OF ATTAINING A PERFECTION IN THE ART----WHAT AN ADEPT IS----OF THE CABALA----THE ROSIE CRUCIANS ADEPTISTS----POSSIBILITY OF BEING AN ADEPT----LIKEWISE, THAT THE LAPIS PHILOSOPHORUM EXISTS IN NATURE, AND THAT PROVED BY SUFFICIENT AUTHORITY, AND THAT THEY ARE NOT ALL IMPOSTORS WHO ARE ALCHYMISTS, OR PRETEND TO IT----THE MADNESS OF THE SCHOOLS PROVED, AND THE FOOLISHNESS OF THEIR WISDOM----THE TRIUMPH OF CHEMICAL PHILOSOPHY, OR THE HERMETIC ART PREFERABLE TO ANY OTHER.

IT is not necessary here to enter into a long detail of the merits of Alchymical Authors and Philosophers ; suffice it to say, that Alchymy, the grand touch-stone of natural wisdom, is of Divine origin : it was brought down from Heaven by the Angel Uriel. Zoroaster, the first philosopher by fire, made pure gold from all the seven metals ; he brought the sun ten times brighter from the bed of Saturn, and fixed it with the moon, who thereby copulating, begot a numerous offspring of an immortal nature, a pure living spiritual sun, burning in the refulgency of its own divine light, a seed of a sublime and fiery nature, a vigorous progenitor. This Zoroaster was the father of alchymy, illumined divinely from above ; he knew every thing, yet seemed to know nothing ; his precepts of art were left in hieroglyphics, yet in such sort that none but the favourites of Heaven ever reaped benefit thereby. He was the first who engraved the pure Cabala in most pure gold, and, when he died, resigned it to his Father who liveth eternally, yet begot him not : that Father gives it to his sons, who follow the precepts of Wisdom with vigilance, ingenuity, and industry, and with a pure, chaste, and free mind.

Hermes, Trismegistus, Geber, Artephius, Bacon, Helmont, Lully, and Basil Valentine, have written most profoundly, yet abstrusely, and all declare not the thing sought for. Some say they were forbid ; others that they declared it obviously and intelligibly, yet some few little points they kept to
themselves

themselves. However far off the main point they lead us, of this be sure,—that something valuable is to be drained, as it were, out of each.

Geber is good---Artephius is better---but Flammel is best of all ;---and better still than these is the instructions we give ; for with them a man (following our directions) shall never want gold ; therefore to be an adept is possible, but first " seek the kingdom of God, and all these things shall be added unto you." This is truth incontrovertible, and herein lies a vast secret--- "seek and ye shall find ; "---but remember, whatsoever ye ask, that shall ye receive.

The cabala, in its utmost purity, is contained in the many precepts given in this book. The cabala enables us to understand---to bring our understandings to act, and, by that means, to attain knowledge ;---knowledge makes us the children of God---God makes whom he pleases adepts in wisdom. To be an adept, according to God's will, is no contemptible calling.

The noble and virtuous Brethren of the Rosy Cross holds this truth sacred--- that " Virtue flies from no man ; " therefore how desirable a thing is Virtue. She teaches us, first, wisdom, then charity, love, mercy, faith, and constancy ; all these appertain to Virtue ; therefore it is physically possible for any well-inclined man to become an adept, provided he lays aside his pride of reasoning, all obstinacy, blindness, hypocrisy, incredulity, superstition, deceit, &c.

An adept, therefore, is one who not only studies to do God's will upon earth, in respect of his moral and religious duties ; but who studies, and ardently prays to his benevolent Creator to bestow on him wisdom and knowledge from the fulness of his treasury ; and he meditates, day and night, how he may attain the true *aqua vita*---how he may be filled with the grace of God ; which, when he is made so happy, his spiritual and internal eye is open to a glorious prospect of mortal and immortal riches :---he wants not *food, raiment,* joy, or any other thing---he is filled with the celestial spiritual manna---he enjoys the marrow and fat things of the earth---he treads the wine-press, not of the *wrath,* but of the *mercy* of God---he *lives* to the glory of God, *and dies* saying " Holy, holy, holy Lord of Sabaoth ! blessed is thy name, now and for evermore ! Amen."

Book I.　　　　　　　　　　　　　　　　　　　　Therefore,

Therefore, to be an adept, as we have before hinted, is to know thyself, fear God, and love thy neighbour as thyself; and by this thou shalt come to the fulfilment of thy desires, O, man; but by no other means under the scope of Heaven.

When thy soul shall be made drunk by the divine ambrosial nectar, then shall thy understanding be more clear than the noontide sun;---then, by thy strong and spiritualized intellectual eye, shalt thou see into the great treasury of Nature, and thou shalt praise God with thy whole heart;---then wilt thou see the folly of the world; and thou shalt unerringly accomplish thy desire, and shalt possess the true Philosophers' stone, to the profit of thy neighbour. I say, thou shalt visibly and sensibly, according to thy corporal faculties; not imaginary, not delusively, but real.

Helmont, an author of no mean repute, avouches that he has actually seen the stone which converts base metals into gold; that he has seen it with his eyes, and handled it with his fingers : taken from his own relation of the fact; notwithstanding Kircher's declamation against the possibility of obtaining it, noting them all who professed alchymy to be a set of impostors and jugglers, giving no better an exposition of their process of transmutation than this---" An Alchymist," says Kircher, " procures or desires a crucible to be brought, wherein is put lead or any other base metal, which, while in fusion, he (the Alchymist) stirs about with an iron rod, and then," he says, " he drops in, from between his fingers, a bit of gold; and after stirring up for some time, and essay being made, gold is found." This is, indeed, a very lame method of exploding alchymy; but, however, to leave Kircher as much in the dark as he was, we shall give you Van Helmont's declaration, a philosopher of much greater note than this pseudo-chemist Kircher. Van Helmont says---" I have divers times handled that stone with my hands, and have seen a real transmutation of saleable quicksilver with mine eyes, which, in proportion, did exceed the powder which made the gold in some thousand degrees.

" It was of the colour that is in saffron, being weighty in its powder, and shining like bruised glass, when it should be the less exactly beaten. But there was once given unto me the fourth part of one grain, (I call, also, a

grain

grain the six hundredth part of an ounce). This powder I involved in wax, scraped off a certain letter, lest, in casting it into the crucible, it should be dispersed, through the smoak of the coals; which pellet of wax I afterwards cast into the three-cornered vessel of a crucible upon a pound of quicksilver, hot and newly bought; and presently the whole quicksilver, with some little noise, stood still from flowing, and resided like a lump; but the heat of that *argent vive* was as much as might forbid melted lead from recoagulating. The fire being straightway after increased under the bellows, the metal was melted; the which, the vessel of fusion being broken, I found to weigh eight ounces of the most pure gold.

"Therefore, a computation being made, a grain of that powder doth convert nineteen thousand two hundred grains of impure and volatile metal, which is obliterable by the fire, into true gold.

"For that powder, by uniting the aforesaid quicksilver unto itself, preserved the same, at one instant, from an eternal rust, putrefaction, death, and torture of the fire, howsoever most violent it was, and made it as an immortal thing, against any vigour or industry of art and fire, and transchanged it into the virgin purity of gold; at leastwise one only fire of coals is required herein."

By which we see that so learned and profound a philosopher as Van Helmont could not so easily have been made to believe that there existed a possibility of transmutation of base metals into pure gold, without he had actually proved the same by experiment.

Again, let the standing monuments of Flammel's liberal bounty to the poor, through this mean, to be seen at Paris every day, stand as a testimony to the truth of the existing possibility of transmutation. Likewise, Helmont mentions a stone that he saw, and had in his possession, which cured all disorders, the plague not excepted. I shall relate the circumstance in his own words, which are as follow :---

"There was a certain Irishman, whose name was Butler, being some time great with James, King of England, he being detained in the prison of the Castle of Vilvord; and taking pity on one Baillius, a certain Franciscan Monk, a most famous preacher of Gallo-Britain, who was also imprisoned,

having

having an erisipelas in his arm; on a certain evening, when the Monk did almost despair, he swiftly tinged a certain little stone in a spoonful of almond-milk, and presently withdrew it thence. So he says to the keeper---'Reach this supping to that Monk; and how much soever he shall take thereupon, he shall be whole, at least within a short hour's space.'---Which thing even so came to pass, to the great admiration of the keeper and the sick man, not knowing from whence so sudden health shone upon him, seeing that he was ignorant that he had taken any thing: for his left arm, being before hugely swollen, fell down as that it could scarcely be discerned from the other. On the morning following, I, being entreated by some great men, came to Vilvord, as a witness of his deeds; therefore I contracted a friendship with Butler.

" Soon afterwards, I saw a poor old woman, a laundress, who, from the age of sixteen years, had laboured with an intolerable megrim, cured in my presence. Indeed he, by the way, lightly dipped the same little stone in a spoonful of oil of olives, and presently cleansed the same stone by licking it with his tongue, and laid it up into his snuff-box; but that spoonful of oil he poured into a small bottle of oil, whereof one only drop he commanded to be anointed on the head of the aforesaid old woman, who was thereby straightway cured, and remained whole; which I attest I was amazed, as if he was become another Midas; but he, smiling, said---

' My most dear friend, unless thou come hitherto, so as to be able, by one only remedy, to cure *every disease*, thou shalt remain in thy *young beginnings*, however *old* thou shalt become.'---I easily assented to this, because I had learned that from the secrets of Paracelsus; and being now more confirmed by sight and hope. But I willingly confess, that that new mode of curing was unaccustomed and unknown to me: I therefore said, that a young Prince of our Court, Viscount of Gaunt, brother to the Prince of Episuoy, of a very great House, was so wholly prostrated by the gout, that he thenceforth lay only on one side, being wretched, and deformed with many knots: he, therefore, taking hold of my right hand, said---'Wilt thou that I cure the young man? I will cure him for thy sake.'---' But,' I replied, ' he is of that obstinacy, that he had rather die, than drink one only medicinal potion.'

' Be

' Be it so,' said Butler; ' for neither do I require any other thing, than that he do, every morning, touch this little stone, thou seest, with the top of his tongue; for after three weeks from thence, let him wash the painful and unpainful knots with his own urine, and thou shalt soon afterwards see him cured, and soundly walking. Go thy ways, and tell him, with joy, what I have said.'

" I therefore, being glad, returned to Brussels, and told him what Butler had said.

" But the Potentate answered---' Go, tell Butler that if he shall restore me as thou hast said, I will give him as much as he shall require;---demand the price, and I will willingly sequester that which is deposited for his security.--- And when I declared the thing to Butler, on the day following, he was very wrath, and said---' That Prince is mad, or witless and miserable, and there-fore will I never help him : for neither do I stand in need of his money--- neither do I yield---nor am I inferior to him.'---Nor could I ever induce him, afterwards, to perform what before he had promised ; wherefore I began to doubt whether the things I had before seen were dreams.

" It happened, in the mean time, that a friend, overseer and master of the glass-furnace at Antwerp, being exceeding fat, most earnestly requested of Butler that he might be freed from his fatness ; unto whom Butler offered a small piece of that little stone, that he might once every morning lick, or speedily touch it with the top of his tongue : and, within three weeks, I saw his breast made more strait, or narrow, by one span, and him to have lived no less whole afterwards. Wherefore I began again to believe that the afore-said gouty Prince might have been cured, according to the manner Butler had promised.

" In the mean time, I sent to Vilvord, to Butler, for a remedy, in the case of poison given me by a secret enemy ; for I miserably languished---all my joints were pained ; and my pulse, vehement, being at length become an intermitting one, did accompany the faintings of my mind, and extinguishment of my strength.

" Butler,

" Butler, being still detained in prison, commanded my household-servant, whom I had sent, that forthwith he should bring unto him a small bottle of oil of olives ; and his little stone, aforesaid, being tinged therein, as at other times, he sent that oil unto me ; and told the servant, that with one only small drop of the oil, I should anoint only one place of the pain, or all the places, if I would ; the which I did, and yet felt no help thereby.   In the mean time, my enemy, according to his lot, being about to die, bade that pardon should be craved of me for his sin ; so I knew that I had taken poison, the which I suspected ; and therefore, also, I procured with all care to extinguish the slow venom, which, through the grace of God favouring me, I escaped.

" Seeing that, afterwards, many other cures were performed upon certain gentlewomen, I asked Butler why so many women should be cured, but that I (while that I sharply conflicted with death itself, being also environed with pains of all my joints and organs) should not feel any ease ?---But he asked with what disease I had laboured ?---And when he understood that poison had given a beginning to the disease, he said,---that, as the cause had come from within to without, the oil ought to be taken into the body, or the stone to be touched with the tongue ; because the grief being cherished within, it was not local or external ; and also observed, that the oil did, by degrees, uncloath itself with the efficacy of healing, because the little stone being lightly tinged in it, it had not pithily charged the oil throughout its whole body, but had only ennobled it with a delible or obliterable besprinkling of its odour : for truly that stone did present, in the eyes and tongue, sea-salt spread abroad, or rarified ; and it is sufficiently known that salt is not to be very intimately mixed with oil.

" This same man, also, cured an Abbess, who, for eighteen years, had had her right arm swelled, with an entire deprivation of motion, and the fingers thereof stiff and unmoveable, only by the touching of her tongue with this admirable stone.

" But very many being present witnesses of these same wonders, did suspect some hidden sorcery, or diabolical craft ; for the common people have it for an ancient custom, that whatsoever honest thing their ignorance has determined

not

not to comprehend, they do, for a privy shift of their ignorance, refer the same to be the juggling of an evil spirit. But I could never decline so far, because the remedy was supposed to be natural; for neither words, ceremonies, nor any other suspected thing, was required. For neither is it lawful, according to man's power of understanding, to refer the glory of God, shewn forth in Nature, unto the devil. For none of those people had required aid of Butler, as from necromancy any way suspected; yea, the thing was at first made trial of with smiling, and without faith and confidence; yet this easy method of curing shall long remain suspected by many; for the wit of the vulgar being inconstant and idle, they do more readily consecrate so great a bounty of restitution unto diabolical contrivance, than to Divine goodness, the framer, lover, saviour, refresher of human nature, and the father of the poor. And these vile prejudices are not only inherent in the common people, but also in those that are learned, who rashly search into the beginning of healing, being not yet instructed, or observing the common and blockish rules; because they are always wise as children, who have never gone over their mother's threshold, being afraid of every fable. For they who have not hitherto known the whole circuit of diseases to be included within the spirit of life, which maketh the assault; or if they hereafter, reading my studies by the way, shall imprint on themselves this moment or concernment of healing; nevertheless, because they have been already before accustomed from the very beginnings of their studies, to the precepts of the humorists, they will easily, at length, depart from me, and leap back to the favourite bigotry and ancient opinions of the schools."

But now we will hasten to the manner of preparation necessary to qualify a man for the attainment of these sublime gifts.

Of

*Of the Preparation of a Man to qualify him for the Search of this Treasure;
and of the first Matter (prima materia) of the Stone.*

LESSON I.

THE preparation for this work is simply this :---Learn to cast away from
thee all vile affections---all levity and inconstancy of mind ; let all thy
dealings be free from deceit and hypocrisy ; avoid the company of vain young
men ; hate all profligacy, and profane speaking.

LESSON II.

Keep thy own, and thy neighbours' secrets ; court not the favours of the
rich ; despise not the poor, for he who does will be poorer than the poorest.

LESSON III.

Give to the needy and unfortunate what little thou canst spare ; for he that
has but little, whatever he spares to the miserable, God shall amply reward him.

LESSON IV.

Be merciful to those who offend thee, or who have injured thee ; for what
must that man's heart be, who would take heavy vengeance on a slight offence ?
Thou shalt forgive thy brother until seventy times seven.

LESSON V.

Be not hasty to condemn the actions of others, lest thou shouldst, the
next hour, fall into the very same error ; despise scandal and tattling ; let thy
words be few.

LESSON VI.

Study day and night, and supplicate thy Creator that he would be pleased to grant thee knowledge and understanding; and that the pure spirits may have communication with, and influence, in thee.

LESSON VII.

Be not overcome with drunkenness; for, be assured, that half the evils that befall mankind originate in drunkenness: for too great a quantity of strong liquors deprive men of their reason; then, having lost the use of the faculty of their judgment, they immediately become the recipient of all evil influences, and are justly compared to weathercocks, that are driven hither and thither by every gust of wind; so those who drown the reasonable power, are easily persuaded to the lightest and most frivolous pursuits, and, from these, to vices more gross and reprobate; for the ministers of darkness have never so favourable an opportunity of insinuating themselves into the minds and hearts of men, as when they are lost in intoxication. I pray you to avoid this dreadful vice.

LESSON VIII.

Avoid gluttony, and all excess---it is very pernicious, and from the Devil: these are the things that constantly tempt man, and by which he falls a prey to his spiritual adversary; for he is rendered incapable of receiving any good or divine gift. Besides, the divine and angelic powers or essences delight not to be conversant about a man who is defiled, and stinking with debauchery and excess.

LESSON IX.

Covet not much gold, but learn to be satisfied with enough; for to desire more than enough, is to offend the Deity.

Book I.　　　　　　　　　　　　　　　　　　　　　　　　LESSON

LESSON X.

Read often these ten preparatory Lessons to fit thee for the great work, and for the receiving of higher things; for the more pure thou art in heart and mind, by so much quicker shall you perceive those high secrets we teach, and which are entirely hid from the discernment of the vicious and depraved, because it never can happen that such a source of treasure can be attained merely to satisfy our more gross, earthly, and vain desires and inclinations, because here nothing must be thought to be grasped, or wrested out of this book, but to the fulfilling of a good end and purpose. When thou shalt have so far purified thy heart, as we have spoken is indispensably necessary for the receiving of every good thing, thou shalt then see with other eyes than thou dost at present---thy spiritual eye will be opened, and thou shalt read man as plain as thou wilt our books; but, for all this, depend not on the strength of thy own wisdom, for even then, when we think our hearts secure, if we do not watch them that they sleep not, the Devil, or his ministers, immediately take us at this unguarded moment, and tempts us into the actual commission of some sin or other: either he excites our appetite for lust and concupiscence, or any other deadly sin; therefore, using our blessed Redeemer's words---" What I say unto you, I say unto you all---watch!"

Perhaps, I do not doubt but, there are some that will say, when they look at our works, this fellow is all rant, all preaching---he tells us what we knew before as well as himself. To such I say, let them read our book but twice; if they do not gather something that they will acknowledge precious, (nay, be *convinced* that it is precious, to their own satisfaction) I will burn these writings, and they shall be no more remembered by me.

To conclude this Part: we say that the First Matter (*Prima Materia*) Adam brought with him out of Paradise, and left it, as an inheritance, to us his successors; had he remained in his original purity, he would have been permitted to have used it himself; but the eternal fiat. was passed, that he was to " earn his bread by the sweat of his brow;" therefore he could not effect what was afterwards performed by some of his offspring.

Hermes

Hermes Trismegistus, that ancient philosopher, wrote touching the attainment of this stone, which he pronounced to be of all benefit to man, and one of the greatest blessings he could possess; and although his writings contain much of the excellency of truth, being wrapped up in such symbolical figures, it renders them exceedingly difficult to be understood, yet, if comprehended, they, no doubt, contain some very great secrets by which mortal man may profit.

Now it belongs to our purpose to know *what it is* from which we must extract the first matter of this stone, to go on with our process, because we must have materials to work upon; for all philosophers agree that, the first matter being found, we may proceed without much difficulty. *For the first matter*, (I shall speak as plainly as possible) first, the grand question in debate is---Where is it to be found?---I say it is to be found in ourselves. We all possess this first matter, from the beggar to the king; every mothers' son carries it about him; and, could our ingenious chemists but find a process for the extracting, how well would all their labours be repaid. The next question naturally comes to us---How are we to draw, or attract the secret matter of the stone out of ourselves?---Not by any common means; and yet it is to be drawn into very action, and that by the most simple means, and in a manner that the attaining of the philosophers' stone would very soon follow it. I pray you, my friend, look into thyself, and endeavour to find out in what part of thy composition is the *prima materia* of the *lapis philosophorum*, or out of what part of thy substance can the first matter of our stone be drawn out. Thou sayest, it must either be in the *hair*, *sweat*, or *excrement*. I say in none of these thou shalt ever be able to find it, and yet thou shalt find it in thyself.

Many great philosophers and chemists, whom I have the pleasure to know, affirm that, admitting of the possibility of transmutation, it (*i. e.* the *first matter*) must be taken from the purest gold. To this I say it must not; neither has it any thing at all to do with extrinsical gold. They will say then that the pure ens of gold may be drawn from gold itself. True, it may so; but then I would ask if they could ever produce more gold than

that

that out of which the soul or essence was extracted; if they have, they have indeed found out a secret beyond the powers of our comprehension; because it is against reason to suppose that if a pound of gold yields a drachm of the soul or essence, that that only will tinge any more than a pound of purified lead, or ☿ ; because we have tried various experiments, and I have, in some of my first essays, turned both lead and mercury into good gold; but no more than that out of which the soul was extracted. But, however, not to lose our time in vain and ridiculous disputation, know that whatever prodigious things or experiments have been tried with respect to the first matter, by external subjects, either in the mineral, animal, or vegetable kingdoms, as they are called, I say in US is the power of all wonderful things, which the supreme Creator has, of his infinite mercy, implanted in our souls; out of her is to be extracted the first matter, the true *argent vive*, the ☿ of the philosophers, the true ens of ☉, viz. a spiritual living gold, or waterish mercury, or first matter, which, by being maturted, is capable o f transmuting a thousand pts. of impure metal into good and perfect gold, which endure fire, test, or cupel.

_____

PART II.

OF THE MANNER OF EXTRACTING THE FIRST MATTER OF THE PHILOSOPHERS' STONE, AND THE USE IT IS PUT TO IN PURIFYING THE IMPERFECT METALS, AND TRANSMUTING THEM INTO GOOD GOLD.

LESSON XI.

TAKE the foregoing instructions as thy principal instrument, and know that our soul has the power, when the body is free, as we before said, of any pollution, the heart void of malice and offence; I say the soul is then a free agent, and has the power, spiritually and magically, to act upon any matter whatsoever; therefore I said the first matter is in the soul; and the extracting of it, is to bring the dormant power of the pure, living, breathing spirit and eternal soul into act. Note well that every agent has its power of acting upon

its

its patient. Every essence that is distilled forth is received into a recipient, but that recipient must first be made clean. Even so must the soul and heart of man : the vile affections must be thrown away, and trampled under foot ; then shalt thou be able to proceed_ in thy work, which do in the manner following.

LESSON XII.

The expence thou must be at will be but a trifle : all the instruments necessary are but three, viz. a crucible, an egg philosophical, and a retort with its receiver.   Put your fine gold, in weight about 5 dwts., file it up, put it into your philosophic egg, pour upon it the twice of its weight of the best Hungarian ☿, close up the egg with an Hermetic seal, put it for three months in horse-dung, take it out at the end of that time, and see what kind of form thy gold and ☿ has assumed ; take it out, pour on it half its weight of good spirit of sal ammon., set them in a pot full of sand over the fire in the retort, let them distil into a pure essence, add to one pt. of this ☿ two pts. of thy water of life, or *prima materia*, put them into thy philosophical egg, and

LESSON XIII.

set them into horse-dung for another three months ; then take them out, and see what thou hast---a pure etherial essence, which is the living gold ; pour this pure spiritual liquor upon a drachm of molten fine gold, and you will find that which will satisfy thy hunger and thirsting after this secret; for the increase of thy gold will seem to thee miraculous, as indeed it is.   Take it to a jeweller's or goldsmith's ; let him try it in thy presence, and thou wilt have reason to bless God for his mercy to thee.   Do thy duty as he has commanded thee, and use all the benefit thou shalt receive, in actions worthy of thy nature.

LESSON XIV.

When thy spiritual eye is opened, and thou shalt begin to see to what end thou wert created, thou shalt want no necessary thing either for thy comfort or
support ;

support; only keep in the rules we have prescribed in the beginning of this little treatise---Fear God, and love thy neighbour as thyself; be not hasty to reveal any secrets thou mayest learn, for the good spirits, both day and night, will be thy instructors, and will continually reveal thee many secrets. Think not that thou canst either profit or benefit so much by the instruction of those who profess great advantages in classical education and high schooling; be assured they are, in spiritual knowledge, much in the dark : for he who desires not spiritual knowledge cannot attain it by any means, but by, first, coming to God ; secondly, by purifying his own heart ; thirdly, by submitting himself to the will of the Holy Spirit, to guide and direct him in all truth, to the attaining of all knowledge, both human and divine; and by arrogating nothing to our own power or strength, but by referring all to the mercy and goodness of God.---*Amen.*

THE

MAGUS;

OR,

CELESTIAL INTELLIGENCER.

CONTAINING

THE CONSTELLATORY PRACTICE,

OR

TALISMANIC MAGIC.

SHEWING

The true Properties of the Elements, Meteors, Stars, Planets, &c. &c. ; likewise the Nature of Intelligences, Spirits, Dæmons, and Devils ; the Construction and Composition of all Sorts of Magic Seals, Images, Rings, Glasses, Pictures, &c, &c. ; the Power and Composition of Numbers, Mathematical Figures, and Characters of Spirits both good and evil.

THE WHOLE OF THE ABOVE ILLUSTRATED BY A GREAT VARIETY OF

Beautiful Figures, Types, Letters, Seals, Images, Magic Characters, &c.

FORMING A COMPLETE SYSTEM OF

DELIGHTFUL KNOWLEDGE AND ABSTRUSE SCIENCE;

Such as is warranted never before to have been published in the English Language.

BY FRANCIS BARRETT,

STUDENT OF CHEMISTRY, OCCULT PHILOSOPHY, THE CABALA, &c. &c. &c.

1801.

PART THE SECOND.

==

CHAP. I.

OF THE FOUR ELEMENTS AND THEIR NATURAL QUALITIES.

I T is necessary that we should know and understand the nature and quality of the four elements, in order to our being perfect in the principles and ground-work of our studies in the Talismanic, or Magical Art.

Therefore, there are four elements, the original grounds of all corporeal things, viz. fire, earth, water, and air, of which elements all inferior bodies are compounded; not by way of being heaped up together, but by transmutation and union; and when they are destroyed, they are resolved into elements. But there are none of the sensible elements that are pure; but they are, more or less, mixed, and apt to be changed the one into the other: even as earth, being moistened and dissolved, becomes *water*, but the same being made thick and hard, becomes earth again; and being evaporated through heat it passes into air, and that being kindled into fire, and this being extinguished, into air again, but being cooled after burning, becomes earth again, or else stone, or sulphur; and this is clearly demonstrated by lightning. Now every one of these elements have two specifical properties: the former whereof it retains as proper to itself; in the other, as a mean, it agrees with that which comes directly after it. For fire is hot and dry---earth, cold and dry;---water, cold and moist---and air, hot and moist. And so in this manner the elements, according to two contrary qualities, are opposite one to the other: as fire to water, and earth to air. Likewise, the elements are contrary one to the other on another account: two are heavy, as earth and water---and the others are light, as fire and air; therefore the Stoics called the former, passives---but the latter, actives. And Plato distinguishes them after another manner, and

BOOK I.   assigns

assigns to each of them three qualities, viz. to the fire, brightness, thinness, and motion---to the earth, darkness, thickness, and quietness; and, according to these qualities, the elements of fire and earth are contrary. Now the other elements borrow their qualities from these, so that the air receives two qualities from the fire,---thinness, and motion; and the earth one, viz. darkness. In like manner water receives two qualities of the earth,---darkness and thickness; and the fire one, viz. motion. But fire is twice as thin as air, thrice more moveable, and four times brighter; the air is twice more bright, thrice more thin, and four times more moveable. Therefore, as fire is to air, so is air to water, and water to the earth; and again, as the earth is to the water, so is water to air, and air to fire. And this is the root and foundation of all bodies, natures, and wonderful works; and he who can know, and thoroughly understand these qualities of the elements, and their mixtures, shall bring to pass wonderful and astonishing things in magic.

Now each of these elements have a threefold consideration, so that the number of four may make up the number of twelve; and, by passing by the number of seven into ten, there may be a progress to the supreme unity upon which all virtue and wonderful things do depend. Of the first order are the pure elements, which are neither compounded, changed, or mixed, but are incorruptible; and not OF which, but THROUGH which, the virtues of all natural things are brought forth to act. No man is able fully to declare their virtues, because they can do all things upon all things. He who remains ignorant of these, shall never be able to bring to pass any wonderful matter.

Of the second order are elements that are compounded, changeable, and impure; yet such as may, by art, be reduced to their pure simplicity; whose virtue, when they are thus reduced, doth, above all things, perfect all occult and common operations of Nature; and these are the foundation of the whole of Natural Magic.

Of the third order, are those elements which originally and of themselves are not elements, but are twice compounded, various and changeable into another. These are the infallible *medium*, and are called the *middle nature*, or soul of the middle nature; very few there are that understand the deep mys-

teries

teries thereof. In them is, by means of certain numbers, degrees, and orders, the perfection of every effect in what thing soever, whether *natural, celestial,* or supercelestial : they are full of wonders and mysteries, and are operative as in Magic natural, so divine. For from these, through them, proceeds the binding, loosing, and transmutation of all things---the knowledge and foretelling of things to come---also, the expelling of evil, and the gaining of good spirits. Let no one, therefore, without these three sorts of elements, and the true knowledge thereof, be confident that he can work any thing in the Occult Science of Magic and Nature.

But whosoever shall know how to reduce those of one order into another, impure into pure, compounded into simple, and shall understand distinctly the *nature, virtue,* and power of them, in number, degrees, and order, without dividing the substance, he shall easily attain to the knowledge and perfect operation of all natural things, and celestial secrets likewise ; and this is the perfection of the Cabala, which teaches all these before mentioned ; and, by a perfect knowledge thereof, we perform many rare and wonderful experiments.

CHAP. II.

OF THE PROPERTIES AND WONDERFUL NATURE OF FIRE AND EARTH.

THERE are two things, (says Hermes) viz. fire and earth, which are sufficient for the operation of all wonderful things : the former is active, and the latter passive. Fire, in all things, and through all things, comes and goes away bright ; it is in all things bright, and at the same time occult, and unknown. When it is by itself (no other matter coming to it, in which it should manifest its proper action) it is boundless and invisible ; of itself sufficient for every action that is proper to it ;---itself is one, and penetrates through all things ; also spread abroad in the heavens, and shining. But in the infernal place, straitened, dark, and tormenting ; and in the midway it partakes of both. I is in stones, and is drawn out by the stroke of the steel ; it is in earth, and

causes

causes it, after digging up, to smoke; it is in water, and heats springs and wells; it is in the depths of the sea, and causes it, being tossed with the winds, to be hot; it is in the air, and makes it (as we often see) to burn. And all animals, and all living things whatsoever, as also vegetables, are preserved by heat;---and every thing that lives, lives by reason of the inclosed heat. The properties of the fire that is above, are heat, making all things fruitful; and a celestial light, giving life to all things. The properties of the infernal fire are a parching heat, consuming all things; and darkness; making all things barren. The celestial and bright fire drives away spirits of darkness;---also, this our fire, made with wood, drives away the same, in as much as it hath an analogy with, and is the *vehiculum* of, that superior light; as also of him who saith, "I am the light of the world," which is true fire--- the Father of lights, from whom every good thing that is given comes;--- sending forth the light of his fire, and communicating it first to the sun and the rest of the celestial bodies, and by these, as by mediating instruments, conveying that light into our fire. As, therefore, the spirits of darkness are stronger in the dark---so good spirits, which are angels of lights, are augmented not only by that light (which is divine, of the sun, and celestial), but also by the light of our common fire. Hence it was that the first and most wise institutors of religions and ceremonies, ordained that prayers, singings, and all manner of divine worships whatsoever, should not be performed without lighted candles or torches: hence, also, was that significant saying of Pythagoras---" Do not speak of God without a light!"---And they commanded that, for the driving away of wicked spirits, lights and fires should be kindled by the carcasses of the dead, and that they should not be removed until the expiations were, after a holy manner, performed, and then buried. And the great Jehovah himself, in the old law, commanded that all his sacrifices should be offered with fire and that fire should always be burning upon the altar, which custom the Priests of the Altar did always observe and keep amongst the Romans. Now the basis and foundation of all the elements is the earth; for that is the object, subject, and receptacle of all celestial rays and influences: in it are contained the seeds, and seminal virtues of all things; and therefore, it is said to be

animal,

animal, vegetable, and mineral. It, being made fruitful by the other elements and the heavens, brings forth all things of itself. It receives the abundance of all things, and is, as it were, the first fountain from whence all things spring ;---it is the centre, foundation, and mother of all things. Take as much of it as you please, separated, washed, depurated, and subtilized, and if you let it lie in the open air a little while, it will, being full and abounding with heavenly virtues, of itself bring forth plants, worms, and other living things; also stones, and bright sparks of *metals*. In it are great secrets : if, at any time it shall be purified, by the help of fire,* and reduced into its simple nature by a convenient washing, it is the first matter of our creation, and the truest medicine that can restore and preserve us.

CHAP. III.

OF THE WATER AND AIR.

THE other two elements, viz. water and air, are not less efficacious than the former; neither is Nature wanting to work wonderful things in them. There is so great a necessity of water, that without it nothing can live ---no herb nor plant whatsoever without the moistening of water, can bring forth; in it is the seminary virtue of all things, especially of animals, whose seed is manifestly waterish. The seeds, also, of trees and plants, although they are earthy, must, notwithstanding, of necessity be rotted in water before they can be fruitful; whether they be imbibed with the moisture of the earth, or with dew, or rain, or any other water that is on purpose put to them.--- For Moses writes, that only earth and water can bring forth a living soul; but he ascribes a two-fold production of things to water, viz. of things swimming in the water, and of things flying in the air above the earth ; and

* Agrippa here, speaking of the element of earth being reduced to its utmost simplicity, by being purified by fire and a convenient washing, means, that it is the first and principal ingredient necessary to the production of the Philosopher's stone, either of animals or metals.

that

that those productions that are made in and upon the earth are partly attributed to the very water the same scripture testifies, where it saith, that the plants and the herbs did not grow, because God had not caused it to rain upon the earth. Such is the efficacy of this element of water, that spiritual regeneration cannot be done without it, as Christ himself testified to Nicodemus. Very great, also, is the virtue of it in the religious worship of God, in expiations and purifications; indeed the necessity of it is no less than that of fire. Infinite are the benefits, and divers are the uses, thereof as being that, by virtue of which all things subsist, are generated, nourished, and increased. Hence it was that Thales of Miletus, and Hesiod, concluded that water was the beginning of all things; and said it was the first of all the elements, and the most potent; and that, because it hath the mastery over all the rest. For, as Pliny saith---"Waters swallow up the earth---extinguish flames---ascend on high---and, by the stretching forth of the clouds, challenge the heavens for their own; the same, falling down, becomes the cause of all things that grow in the earth." Very many are the wonders that are done by waters, according to the writings of Pliny, Solinus, and many other historians.

Josephus also makes relation of the wonderful nature of a certain river betwixt Arcea and Raphanea, cities of Syria, which runs with a full channel all the Sabbath-day, and then on a sudden stops, as if the springs were stopped, and all the six days you may pass over it dry-shod; but again, on the seventh day, no man knowing the reason of it, the waters return again, in abundance as before! wherefore the inhabitants thereabout called it the Sabbath-day River) because of the seventh day, which was holy to the Jews.--- The Gospel, also, testifies of a sheep-pool, into which whosoever stepped first after the water was troubled by the Angel, was made whole of whatsoever disease he had. The same virtue and efficacy, we read, was in a spring of the Ionian Nymphs, which was in the territories belonging to the town of Elis, at a village called Heradea, near the river Citheron, which whosoever stepped into, being diseased, came forth whole, and cured of all his diseases. Pausanias also reports, that in Lyceus, a mountain of Arcadia, there was a

spring

spring called Agria, to which, as often as the dryness of the region threatened
the destruction of fruits, Jupiter, Priest of Lyceus, went; and, after the offer-
ing of sacrifices, devoutly praying to the waters of the spring, holding a
bough of an oak in his hand, put it down to the bottom of the hallowed
spring; then, the waters being tronbled, a vapour ascending from thence into
the air, was blown into clouds, which being joined together, the whole heaven was overspread: which being, a little after, dissolved into rain, watered
all the country most wholesomely.---Moreover, Ruffus, a physician of Ephesus,
besides many other authors, wrote strange things concerning the wonders of
waters, which, for aught I know, are found in no other author.

It remains, that I speak of the air.---This is a vital spirit passing through all
beings---giving life and subsistence to all things---moving and filling all
things.   Hence it is that the Hebrew doctors reckon it not amongst the elements; but count it as a medium, or glue, joining things together, and as
the resounding spirit of the world's instrument.   It immediately receives into
itself the influence of all celestial bodies, and then communicates them to the
other elements, as also to all mixed bodies.   Also, it receives into itself, as if
it were a divine looking-glass, the species of all things, as well natural as
artificial; as also of all manner of speeches, and retains them; and carrying
them with it, and entering into the bodies of men, and other animals, through
their pores, makes an impression upon them, as well when they are asleep as
when they are awake, and affords matter for divers strange dreams and divina-
tions.---Hence, they say, it is that a man, passing by a place where a man
was slain, or the carcass newly hid, is moved with fear and dread; because
the air, in that place, being full of the dreadful species of man-slaughter,
doth, being breathed in, move and trouble the spirit of the man with the like
species; whence it is that he becomes afraid.   For every thing that makes a
sudden impression astonishes Nature.   Whence it is that many philosophers
were of opinion, that air is the cause of dreams, and of many other impres-
sions of the mind, through the prolonging of images, or similitudes, or species (which proceed from things and speeches, multiplied in the very air), until
they come to the senses, and then to the phantasy and soul of him that receives
                                                                    them;

them ; which, being freed from cares, and no way hindered, expecting to meet such kind of species, is informed by them. For the species of things, although of their own proper nature they are carried to the senses of men, and other animals in general, may, notwithstanding, get some impression from the heavens whilst they are in the air ; by reason of which, together with the aptness and disposition of him that receives them, they may be carried to the sense of one, rather than of another. And hence it is possible, naturally, and far from all manner of superstition (no other spirit coming between), that a man should be able, in a very small time, to signify his mind unto another man, abiding at a very long and unknown distance from him--- although he cannot precisely give an estimate of the time when it is, yet, of necessity, it must be within twenty-four hours ;---and I, myself, know how to do it, and have often done it. The same also, in time past, did the Abbot Tritemius both know and do.---Also, when certain appearances (not only spiritual, but also natural) do flow forth from things, that is to say, by a certain kind of flowings forth of bodies from bodies, and do gather strength in the air, they shew themselves to us as well through light as motion---as well to the sight as to other senses---and sometimes work wonderful things upon us, as Platonius proves and teacheth. And we see how, by the south-wind, the air is condensed into thin clouds, in which, as in a looking-glass, are reflected representations at a great distance, of castles, mountains, horses, men, and other things, which when the clouds are gone, presently vanish.---And Aristotle, in his Meteors, shews that a rainbow is conceived in a cloud of the air, as in a looking-glass.---And Albertus says, that the effigies of bodies may, by the strength of Nature, in a moist air, be easily represented ; in the same manner as the representations of things are in things.---And Aristotle tells of a man, to whom it happened, by reason of the weakness of his sight, that the air that was near to him became, as it were, a looking-glass to him, and the optic-beam did reflect back upon himself, and could not penetrate the air, so that, whithersoever he went, he thought he saw his own image, with his face towards him, go before him.---In like manner, by the artificialness of some certain looking-glasses, may be produced at a distance, in the air, besides the

looking-

looking-glasses, what images we please; which, when ignorant men see, they think they see the appearances of spirits or souls---when, indeed, they are nothing else but semblances a-kin to themselves, and without life. And it is well-known, if in a dark place, where there is no light but by the coming in of a beam of the sun some where through a little hole, a white paper or plain looking-glass be set up against the light, that there may be seen upon them whatsoever things are done without, being shined upon by the sun. And there is another slight or trick yet more wonderful :---if any one shall take images, artificially painted, or written letters, and, in a clear night, set them against the beams of the full moon, those resemblances being multiplied in the air, and caught upward, and reflected back together with the beams of the moon, another man, that is privy to the thing, at a long distance, sees, reads, and knows them in the very compass and circle of the moon; which art of declaring secrets is, indeed, very profitable for towns and cities that are besieged, being a thing which Pythagoras long since did, and which is not unknown to some in these days; I will not except myself. And all these things, and many more, and much greater than these, are grounded in the very nature of the air, and have their reasons and causes declared in mathematics and optics. And as these resemblances are reflected back to the sight, so also are they, sometimes, to the hearing, as is manifest in echo. But there are many more secret arts than these, and such whereby any one may, at a remarkable distance, hear, and understand distinctly, what another speaks or whispers.

CHAP. IV.

OF COMPOUND, OR MIXED BODIES----IN WHAT MANNER THEY RELATE TO THE ELEMENTS ---AND HOW THE ELEMENTS RELATE TO THE SOULS, SENSES, AND DISPOSITIONS OF MEN.

THE next in order, after the four simple elements, are the four kinds of perfect bodies compounded of them, viz. metals, stones, plants, and animals; and although in the generation of each of these, all the elements combine to-

BOOK I.   gether

gether in the composition, yet every one of them follows and resembles one of the elements which is most predominant : for all stones, being earthy, are naturally heavy, and are so hardened with dryness that they cannot be melted ;---but metals are watery, and may be melted, which naturalists and chemists find to be true, viz. that they are composed or generated of a viscous water, or watery *argent vive*. Plants have such an affinity with the air, that unless they are out in it, and receive its benefit, they neither flourish nor increase. So also animals, as the Poet finely expresses it----

> " Have, in their natures, a most fiery force,
> " And also spring from a celestial source : "

and fire is so natural to them that, being extinguished, they soon die.

Now, amongst stones, those that are dark and heavy, are called *earthy*---those which are transparent, of the *watery element*, as crystal, beryl, and pearls---those which swim upon the water and are spongious, as the pumice-stone, sponge, and sophus, are called airy---and those are attributed to the element of fire, out of which fire is extracted, or which are resolved into fire ; as thunder-stones, fire-stones, asbestos. Also, amongst metals ;---lead and silver are earthy ; quicksilver is watery ; copper and tin, airy ; gold and iron, fiery. In plants, also, the roots resemble earth---the leaves, water---flowers, the air---and seed, the fire, by reason of their multiplying spirit. Besides, some are hot, some cold, some moist, others dry, borrowing their names from the qualities of the elements. Amongst animals, also, some are, in comparison of others, earthy, because they live in the very bowels of the earth, as worms, moles, and many other reptiles ; others watery, as fish ; others which always abide in the air, therefore airy ; others, again, fiery, as salamanders, crickets ; and such as are of a fiery heat, as pigeons, ostriches, eagles, lions, panthers, &c. &c.

Now, in animals, the bones resemble earth---vital spirit, the fire---flesh, the air---and humours, the water ; and these humours also resemble the elements, viz. yellow choler, the fire---the blood, the air---phlegm, the water---and

black

black choler, or melancholy, the earth. And, lastly, in the soul itself, the understanding resembles the fire---reason, the air---imagination, the water--- and the senses the earth. And these senses again are divided amongst themselves, according to the elements: for the sight is fiery, because it cannot perceive without the help of fire and light---the hearing is airy, for a sound is made by the striking of the air---the smell and taste resemble water, without the moisture of which there is neither smell nor taste--and, lastly, the feeling is wholly earthly, because it takes gross bodies for its object. The actions, also, and operations of man are governed by the elements: for the earth signifies a slow and firm motion; the water, fearfulness, sluggishness, and remissness in working; air signifies cheerfulness, and an amiable disposition; but fire, a fierce, working, quick, susceptible disposition. The elements are, therefore, the first and original matter of all things; and all things are of and according to them; and they in and through all things diffuse their virtues.

CHAP. V.

THAT THE ELEMENTS ARE IN THE HEAVENS, IN THE STARS, IN DEVILS, ANGELS, INTELLIGENCES, AND, LASTLY, IN GOD HIMSELF.

IN the original and exemplary world, all things are all in all; so also in this corporeal world. And the elements are not only in these inferior things; but are in the heavens, in stars, in devils, in angels, and likewise in God himself, the maker and original example of all things.

Now it must be understood that in these inferior bodies the elements are gross and corruptible; but in the heavens they are, with their natures and virtues, after a celestial and more excellent manner than in sublunary things: for the firmness of the celestial earth is there without the grossness of water; and the agility of air without exceeding its bounds; the heat of fire without burning, only shining, giving light and life to all things by its celestial heat.---Now

amongst

amongst the stars, or planets, some are fiery, as Mars, and the Sun---airy, as
Jupiter, and Venus---watery, as Saturn, and Mercury---and earthy, such as
inhabit the eighth orb, and the Moon (which by many is accounted watery),
seeing that, as if it were earth, it attracts to itself the celestial waters, with
which being imbibed it does, on account of its proximity to us, pour forth and
communicate to our globe.

There are, likewise, amongst the signs, some fiery, some airy, some watery,
and some earthy.   The elements rule *them*, also, in the heavens, distributing
to them these four threefold considerations of every element, according to their
triplicities, viz. the beginning, middle, and end.

Likewise, devils are distinguished according to the elements : for some are
called earthy devils, others fiery, some airy, and others watery.   Hence, also,
those four infernal rivers : fiery Phlegethon, airy Cocytus, watery Styx, earthy
Acheron.   Also, in the Gospel, we read of comparisons of the elements : as
hell fire, and eternal fire, into which the cursed shall be commanded to go ;---
and in Revelations, of a lake of fire :---and Isaiah, speaking of the damned,
says that the Lord will smite them with corrupt air ;---and in Job, they shall
skip from the waters of the snow to the extremity of heat ; and, in the same,
we read, that the earth is dark, and covered with the darkness of death, and
miserable darkness.

And these elements are placed in the angels of heaven, and the blessed intelligences : there is in them a stability of their essence, which is an earthy
virtue, in which is the stedfast seat of God.   By the Psalmist they are called
waters, where he says---" Who rulest the waters that are higher than the
heavens ;"---also, in them their subtile breath is air, and their love is shining
fire ; hence they are called in Scripture, the wings of the wind ; and, in another place, the Psalmist speaks of them thus---" Who makest angels thy spirits,
and thy ministers a flaming fire ! "---Also, according to the different orders of
spirits or angels, some are fiery, as seraphims, authorities, and powers--- earthy,
as cherubim---watery, as thrones and archangels---airy, as dominions and
principalities.

                                                                And

And do we not read of the original Maker of all things, that the earth shall be opened and bring forth a Saviour?---Likewise it is spoken of the same, that he shall be a fountain of living water, cleansing and regenerating; and the same spirit breathing the breath of life; and the same, according to Moses' and Paul's testimony---*a consuming fire.*

That the elements are, therefore, to be found every where, and in all things, after their manner, no man will dare to deny: first, in these inferior bodies, feculent and gross; and in celestials, more pure and clear; but in super-celestials, living, and in all respects blessed. Elements, therefore, in the exemplary world, are ideas of things to be produced; in intelligences, they are distributed powers; in the heavens, they are virtues; and in inferior bodies, are gross forms.

CHAP. VI.

THAT THE WISDOM OF GOD WORKS BY THE MEDIUM OF SECOND CAUSES (I. E. BY THE INTELLIGENCES, BY THE HEAVENS, ELEMENTS, AND CELESTIAL BODIES) IS PROVED BEYOND DISPUTE IN THIS CHAPTER.

IT is to be noted, that God, in the first place, is the end and beginning of all virtue: he gives the *seal* of the *ideas* to his servants, *the intelligences,* who, as faithful officers, *sign* all things entrusted to them with an *ideal virtue;* the heavens and stars, as instruments, disposing the matter, in the mean while, for the receiving of those forms which reside in Divine Majesty, and to be conveyed by stars. And the Giver of forms distributes them by the ministry of his intelligences, which he has ordained as rulers and comptrollers over his works; to whom such a power is entrusted, in things committed to them, that so all virtue in stones, herbs, metals, and all other things, may come from the intelligences, the governors. Therefore the form and virtue of things come first from the *ideas*---then from the ruling and governing intelligences---then from the aspects of the heavens disposing---and, lastly, from the tempers of
the

the elements disposed, answering the influences of the heavens, by which the elements themselves are ordered or disposed. These kinds of operations, therefore, are performed in these inferior things by express forms; and in the heavens, by disposing virtues; in intelligences, by mediating rules; in the original cause, by *ideas* and exemplary forms; all which must of necessity agree in the execution of the effect and virtue of every thing.

There is, therefore, a wonderful virtue and operation in every herb and stone, but greater in a star; beyond which, even from the governing intelligences, every thing receives and obtains many things for itself, especially from the Supreme Cause, with whom all things mutually and exactly correspond, agreeing in an harmonious consent.

Therefore there is *no other cause* of the necessity of effects, than the connection of all things with the First Cause, and their correspondency with those divine patterns and eternal ideas, whence every thing hath its determinate and particular place in the exemplary world, from whence it lives and receives its original being; and every virtue of herbs, stones, metals, animals, words, speeches, and all things that are of God, are placed there.

Now the First Cause (which is God), although he doth, by intelligences and the heavens, work upon these inferior things, does sometimes (these mediums being laid aside, or their officiating being suspended) work those things immediately by himself---which works are then called miracles. But whereas secondary causes do, by the command and appointment of the First Cause, necessarily act, and are necessitated to produce their effects; if God shall, notwithstanding, according to his pleasure, so discharge and suspend them that they shall wholly desist from the necessity of that command, then they are called the greatest miracles of God. For instance: the fire of the Chaldean furnace did not burn the children; the sun stood still at the command of Joshua, and became retrograde one whole day; also, at the prayer of Hezekiah, it went back ten degrees; and when our Saviour Christ was crucified, it became darkened, though at full moon.

And

And the reason of these operations can by no rational discourse, no magic or science, occult or profound soever, be found out or understood; but are to be learned by Divine oracles only.*

CHAP. VII.

OF THE SPIRIT OF THE WORLD.

NOW seeing that the soul is the essential form, intelligible and incorruptible, and is the first mover of the body, and is moved of itself; but that the body, or matter, is of itself unable and unfit for motion, and does very much degenerate from the soul, it appears that there is need of a more excellent medium :---now such a medium is conceived to be the spirit of the world, or that which some call a quintessence; because it is not from the four elements, but a certain *first thing*, having its being above and beside them. There is, therefore, such a kind of medium required to be, by which celestial souls may be joined to gross bodies, and bestow upon them wonderful gifts. This spirit is, in the same manner, in the body of the world, as our spirit is in our bodies; for as the powers of our soul are communicated to the members of the body by the medium of the spirit, so also the virtue of the soul of the world is diffused, throughout all things, by the medium of the universal spirit; for there is nothing to be found in the whole world that hath not a spark of the virtue thereof. Now this spirit is received into things, more or less, by the rays of the stars, so far as things are disposed, or made fit recipients of it. By this spirit, therefore, every occult property is conveyed into herbs, stones, metals, and animals, through the sun, moon, planets, and through stars higher than the planets. Now this spirit may be more advantageous to us if we knew how to separate it from the elements; or, at least, to use those things chiefly

* The foregoing Chapter, if well considered, will open the intellect to a more easy comprehension of the Magical Science of Nature, &c.; and will facilitate, in a wonderful degree, our studies in these sublime mysteries.

which

which are most abounding with this spirit. For those things in which the spirit is less drowned in a body, and less checked by matter, do much more powerfully and perfectly act, and also more readily generate their like; for in it are all *generative* and *seminal virtues*. For which cause the alchymist endeavours to separate this spirit from gold and silver, which, being rightly separated and extracted, if it shall be afterwards projected upon any metal, turns it into gold or silver; which is no way impossible or improbable, when we consider that by art that may be done in a short time, what Nature, in the bowels of the earth (as in a matrix), perfects in a very long space of time.

CHAP. VIII.

OF THE SEALS AND CHARACTERS IMPRESSED BY CELESTIALS UPON NATURAL THINGS.

ALL stars have their peculiar natures, properties, and conditions, the seals and characters whereof they produce through their rays even in these inferior things, viz. in elements, in stones, in plants, in animals, and their members; whence every thing receives from an harmonious disposition, and from its star shining upon it, some particular seal or character stamped upon it, which is the significator of that star or harmony, containing in it a peculiar virtue, different from other virtues of the same matter, both generically, specifically, and numerically. Every thing, therefore, hath its *character* impressed upon it by its *star* for some peculiar effect, especially by that star which doth principally govern it; and these characters contain in them the particular natures, virtues, and roots of their stars, and produce the like operations upon other things on which they are reflected; and stir up and help the influences of their stars, whether they be planets, or fixed stars and figures, or celestial constellations, viz. as often as they shall be made in a fit matter, and in their due and accustomed times; which the ancient wise men (considering such as laboured much in finding out occult properties of things) did set down, in writing, the images of the stars, their figures, seals, marks, characters, such as Nature herself did describe by the rays of the stars in these inferior bodies: some in

stones,

stones, some in plants, some in joints and knots of trees and their boughs, and some in various members of animals. For the bay-tree, lote-tree, and marigold, are solary herbs, and their roots and knots being cut, they show the characters of the sun ; and in stones the character and images of celestial things are often found. But there being so great a diversity of things, there is only a traditional knowledge of a few things which human understanding is able to reach ; therefore very few of those things are known to us, which the ancient philosophers and chiromancers attained to, partly by reason and partly by experience ; and there yet lie hid many things in the treasury of Nature, which the diligent student and wise searcher shall contemplate and discover.

CHAP. IX.

TREATING OF THE VIRTUE AND EFFICACY OF PERFUMES, OR SUFFUMIGATIONS, AND VA-
POURS ; AND TO WHAT PLANETS THEY ARE PROPERLY AND RIGHTLY ATTRIBUTED.

IT is necessary, before we come to the operative or practical part of Talismanic Magic, to show the compositions of fumes or vapours, that are proper to the stars, and are of great force for the opportunely receiving of celestial gifts, under the rays of the stars---inasmuch as they strongly work upon the air and breath ; for our breath is very much changed by such kind of vapours, if both vapours be of the other like. The air being also, through the said vapours, easily moved, or infected with the qualities of inferiors, or celestial (daily quickly penetrating our breast and vitals), does wonderfully reduce us to the like qualities. Let no man wonder how great things suffumigations can do in the air ; especially when they shall, with Porphyry, consider that, by certain vapours exhaled from proper suffumigations, ærial spirits are raised ; also thunder and lightnings, and the like : as the liver of a cameleon being burnt on the house top, will raise showers and lightnings ; the same effect has the head and throat, if they are burnt with oaken wood. There are some suffumigations under the influences of the stars, that cause images of spirits to appear in the air, or elsewhere : for if coriander, smallage, henbane, and hemlock be made to fume, by invocations spirits will soon come together, being attracted by the vapours which are most congruous to their own natures ; hence they are called the herbs of the spirits. Also it is said, that if a fume be made of the root of the reedy herb sagapen, with the juice of hemlock and henbane, and the herb tapsus barbatus, red sanders, and black poppy, it will likewise make strange shapes appear ; but if a suffume be made of smallage, it chases them away, and destroys their visions. Again, if a perfume is made of calamint, piony, mint, and palma christi, it drives away all evil spirits and vain imaginations. Likewise, by certain fumes, animals are gathered together, and put to flight. Pliny mentions concerning the stone liparis, that, with the fume thereof, all beasts are attracted together. The bones in the upper part of the throat of a hart, being burnt, bring serpents together ; but the horn of the hart, being burnt, chases away the same ; likewise, a fume of peacock's feathers does the same. Also, the lungs of an ass, being burnt, puts all poisonous things to flight ; and the fume of the burnt hoof of a horse drives away mice ; the same does the hoof a mule ; and with the hoof of the left-foot flies are driven away. And if a house, or any place, be smoked with the *gall* of a *cuttle-fish*, made into a confection with red storax, roses, and lignum aloes, and then there be some sea-water or blood cast into that place, the whole house will seem to be full of water or blood.

Now such kind of vapours as these, we must conceive, do infect a body, and infuse a virtue into it which continues long, even as the poisonous vapour of the pestilence, being kept for two years in the walls of a house, infects the inhabitants ; and as the contagion of pest or leprosy lying hid in a garment, will, long after, infect him that wears it.

Now there are certain suffumigations used to almost all our instruments of magic (of which hereafter), such as images, rings, &c. For some of the magicians say, that if any one shall hide gold, or silver, or any other such like precious thing (the moon being in conjunction with the sun), and shall perfume the place with *coriander, saffron, henbane*, smallage, and black poppy, of each the same quantity and bruised together, and tempered with

the

the juice of hemlock, that thing which is so hid shall never be taken away therefrom, but that spirit shall continually keep it; and if any one shall endeavour to take it away by force, they shall be hurt, or struck with a frenzy. And *Hermes* says, there is nothing like the fume of spermaceti for the raising up of spirits; therefore if a fume be made of that, lignum aloes, pepperwort, musk, saffron, and red storax, tempered together with the blood of a lapwing or bat, it will quickly gather airy spirits to the place where it is used; and if it be used above the graves of the dead, it will attract spirits and ghosts thither.

Now the use of suffumigations is this : that whenever we set about making any talisman, image, or the like, under the rule or dominion of any star or planet, we should by no means omit the making of a suffumigation appropriate to that planet or constellation under which we desire to work any effect or wonderful operation; as for instance :---when we direct any work to the sun, we must suffume with solary things; if to the moon, with lunary things; and so of the rest. And we must be careful to observe, that as there is a contrariety, or antipathy, in the natures of the stars and planets and their spirits, so there is also in suffumigations : for there is an antipathy between lignum aloes and sulphur frankincense and quicksilver; and spirits that are raised by the fume of lignum aloes, are laid by the burning of sulphur. For the learned Proclus gives an example of a spirit that appeared in the form of a lion, furious and raging : by setting a white cock before the apparition it soon vanished away; because there is so great a contrariety between a cock and a lion;---and let this suffice for a general observation in these kind of things. We shall proceed with showing distinctly the composition of the several fumes appropriated to the seven planets.

CHAP.

CHAP. X.

OF THE COMPOSITION OF SOME PERFUMES APPROPRIATED TO THE SEVEN PLANETS.

THE SUN. ☉

WE make a suffumigation for the sun in this manner :---

Take of saffron, ambergris, musk, lignum aloes, lignum balsam, the fruit of the laurel, cloves, myrrh, and frankincense; of each a like quantity; all of which being bruised, and mixed together, so as to make a sweet odour, must be incorporated with the brain of an eagle, or the blood of a white cock, after the manner of pills, or troches.

THE MOON. ☽

For the moon, we make a suffume of the head of a frog dried, and the eyes of a bull, the seed of white poppies, frankincense, and camphire, which must be incorporated with menstruous blood, or the blood of a goose.

SATURN. ♄

For saturn take the seed of black poppies, henbane, mandrake root, loadstone, and myrrh, and mix them up with the brain of a cat and the blood of a bat.

JUPITER. ♃

Take the seed of ash, lignum aloes, storax, the gum Benjamin, the lapis lazuli, the tops of peacocks' feathers, and incorporate with the blood of a stork, or swallow, or the brain of a hart.

MARS. ♂

Take uphorbium, bdellium, gum armoniac, the roots of both hellebores, the loadstone, and a little sulphur, and incorporate them altogether with the brain of a hart, the blood of a man, and the blood of a black cat.

VENUS.

VENUS. ♀

Take musk, ambergris, lignum aloes, red roses, and red coral, and make them up with sparrow's brains and pigeon's blood.

MERCURY. ☿

Take mastich, frankincense, cloves, and the herb cinquefoil, and the agate stone, and incorporate them all with the brain of a fox, or weasel, and the blood of a magpie.

GENERAL FUMES OF THE PLANETS.

To Saturn are appropriated for fumes, odoriferous roots : as pepper-wort root, &c., and the frankincense tree. To *Jupiter*, all odoriferous fruits : as nutmegs, cloves, &c. To *Mars*, all odoriferous woods : as sanders, cyprus, lignum balsam, and lignum aloes. To the *Sun*, all gums : as frankincense, mastich benjamin, storax, laudanum, ambergris, and musk. To *Venus*, flowers : as roses, violets, saffron, and the like. To Mercury, all the parings of wood or fruit : as cinnamon, lignum cassia, mace, citron peel, and bay-berries, and whatever seeds are odoriferous. To the Moon, the leaves of all vegetables : as the leaf indum, the leaf of the myrtle, and bay tree. Know, also, that according to the opinion of all magicians, in every good matter (as love, good-will, &c.), there must be a good perfume, odoriferous and pre-cious;---and in evil matters (as hatred, anger, misery, and the like), there must be a stinking fume that is of no worth.

The twelves Signs of the Zodiac also have their proper suffumigations, viz., Aries, *myrrh;* Taurus, *pepper-wort;* Gemini, *mastich;* Cancer, *camphire;* Leo, *frankincense;* Virgo, *sanders;* Libra, *galbanum;* Scorpio, *oppoponax;* Sagittarius, *lignum aloes;* Capricorn, *benjamin;* Aquarius, *euphorbium;* Pisces, *red storax.* But Hermes describes the most powerful fume to be, that which is compounded of the seven aromatics, according to the powers of the seven planets : for it receives from *Saturn*, pepper-wort; from *Jupiter*, nut-

meg

meg; from *Mars*, lignum-aloes; from the *Sun*, mastich; from *Venus*, saffron; from *Mercury*, cinnamon; and from the *Moon*, myrtle.

By a close observation of the above order of suffumigations, conjoined with other things, of which we shall speak hereafter (necessary to the full accomplishment of Talismanic Magic), many wonderful effects may be caused, especially if we keep in eye what was delivered in the first part of our Magic, viz. that the soul of the operator must go along with this; otherwise, in vain is *suffumigation, seal, ring, image, picture, glass*, or any other instrument of magic: seeing that it is not merely the disposition, but the act of the disposition, and firm and powerful intent or imagination that gives the effect.---We shall now hasten to speak, generally, of the construction of rings magical, and their wonderful and potent virtues and operations.

CHAP. XI.

OF THE COMPOSITION AND MAGIC VIRTUE OF RINGS.

RINGS, when they are opportunely made, impress their virtues upon us insomuch that they affect the spirit of him that carries them with gladness or sadness; and render him bold or fearful, courteous or terrible, amiable or hateful; inasmuch, also as they fortify us against * sickness, poisons, enemies, evil spirits, and all manner of hurtful things; and often, where the law has no effect, these little trifles greatly assist and corroborate the troubled spirit of the wearer, and help him, in a wonderful manner, to overcome his adversaries, while they do wonder how it is that they cannot effect any hurtful undertaking against him. These things, I say, are great helps against wrathful, vicious, worldly-minded men, inasmuch as they do terrify, hurt, and render invalid the machinations of those who would otherwise work our misery or destruction. All which we are neither afraid nor ashamed to declare, well knowing that these things will be hid from the wicked and profane, so as that they cannot draw the same into

---

* The Author will engage to teach any that are curious in those studies, the particular composition of Talismanic Rings; whereby they may be enabled to judge themselves of the effects that are to be produced by them.

any

any abuse, or privy mischief toward their neighbour; we having reserved some few things in this art to ourselves---not willing to throw pearls before swine. And however simple and plain we may describe some certain experiments and operations (so as that the great-mouthed school philosophers may mutter or scoff thereat), yet there is nothing delivered in this book but what may be, by an understanding thereof, brought into effect, and, likewise, out of which some good may be derived. But to proceed.

The manner of making of these rings is thus :---when any star ascends in the horoscope (fortunately), with a fortunate aspect or conjunction of the moon, we proceed to take a *stone* and herb, that is under that star, and likewise make a ring of the metal that is corresponding to the star; and in the ring, under the stone, put the herb or root, not forgetting to inscribe the *effect, image, name,* and *character*, as also the proper suffume. But I shall speak more of these in another place, where I speak of images and characters. Therefore, in making of rings magical, these things are unerringly to be observed as we have ordered ;---if any one is willing to work any effect or experiment in magic, he must by no means neglect the necessary circumstances which we have so uniformly delivered. I have read, in Philostratus Jarchus, that a Prince of the Indians bestowed seven rings, marked with the virtues and names of the seven planets, to Appollonius, of which he wore one every day, distinguishing according to the names of the days; by the benefit of which he lived above one hundred and thirty years, as also always retained the beauty of his youth. In like manner, Moses, the Lawgiver and Ruler of the Hebrews, being skilled in the Egyptian Magic, is said, by Josephus, to have made rings of love and oblivion. There was also, as saith Aristotle, among the Cireneans, a ring of Battas, which could procure love and honour. We read, also, that Eudamus, a certain philosopher, made rings against the bites of serpents, bewitchings, and evil spirits. The same doth Josephus relate of Solomon. Also we read, in Plato, that Gygus, King of Lydia, had a ring of wonderful and strange virtues; the seal of which, when he turned it toward the palm of his hand, no body could see him, but he could see all things; by the opportunity of which ring, he ravished the Queen, and slew

the

the King his master, and killed whomsoever he thought stood in his way; and in these villanies nobody could see him; and at length, by the benefit of this ring, he became King of Lydia.*

CHAP. XII.

THAT THE PASSIONS OF THE MIND ARE ASSISTED BY CELESTIALS----AND THAT CONSTANCY OF MIND IS IN EVERY WORK NECESSARY.

THE passions of the mind are much helped, and are helpful, and become most powerful, by virtue of the heaven, as they agree with the heaven---either by any natural agreement, or voluntary election; for, as Ptolemy says, he who chuseth that which is the better, seems to differ nothing from him who hath this of Nature. It conduceth, therefore, very much for the receiving the benefit of the heavens, in any work, if we shall, by the heaven, make ourselves suitable to it in our thoughts, affections, imaginations, elections, deliberations, contemplations, and the like. For such like passions vehemently stir up our spirit to their likeness, and suddenly expose us, and our's, to the superior significators of such like passions; and also, by reason of their dignity and nearness to the superiors, do partake more of the celestials than any material things; for our mind can, through imaginations or reason by a kind of imitation, be so conformed to any star, as suddenly to be filled with the virtues of that star, as if we were a proper receptacle of the influence thereof. Now the contemplating mind, as it withdraws itself from all *sense, imagination, nature,* and *deliberation,* and calls itself back to things separated, effects divers things by faith, which is a firm adhesion, a fixed intention, and vehement application of the worker or receiver to him that co-operates in any thing, and gives power to the work which we intend to do. So that there is

---

* We have above shewn the power and virtue of magical rings; but the particular characters, inscriptions, and images to be made in, or upon them, we refer the student to that chapter treating of " The Composition of various Talismans; " in which we have described exactly the express methods of perfecting them.

made

made, as it were, in us the image of the virtue to be received, and the thing
to be done in us, or by us. We must, therefore, in every work and application of things, *affect vehemently*, imagine, hope, and believe strongly, for
that will be a great help. And it is verified amongst physicians, that a strong
belief, and an undoubted hope, and love towards the physician, conduce much
to health, yea more sometimes than the medicine itself; for the same that the
efficacy and virtue of the medicine works, the same doth the strong imagination of the physician work, being able to change the qualities of the body of
the sick, especially when the patient places much confidence in the physician,
by that means disposing himself for the receiving the virtue of the physician,
and physic. Therefore, he that works in magic must be of a constant belief,
be credulous, and not at all doubt of the obtaining of the effect; for as a firm
and strong belief doth work wonderful things, although it be in false works---
so distrust and doubting doth dissipate and break the virtue of the mind of the
worker, which is the medium betwixt both extremes; whence it happens that
he is frustrated of the desired influence of the superiors, which could not be
enjoined and united to our labours without a firm and solid virtue of our
mind.

CHAP. XIII.

HOW MAN'S MIND MAY BE JOINED WITH THE MIND OF INTELLIGENCES AND CELESTIALS AND TOGETHER WITH THEM, IMPRESS CERTAIN WONDERFUL VIRTUES UPON INFERIOR THINGS.

THE philosophers, especially the Arabians, say, that man's mind, when
it is most intent upon any work, through its passion and effects, is joined with
the mind of the stars and intelligences, and, being so joined, is the cause that
some wonderful virtue be infused into our works and things; and this, as because there is in it an apprehension and power of all things, so because all
things have a natural obedience to it, and of necessity an efficacy, and more

to that which desired them with a strong desire. And according to this is verified the art of characters, images, enchantments, and some speeches, and many other wonderful experiments, to every thing which the mind affects. By this means, whatsoever the mind of him that is in vehement love affects, hath an efficacy to cause love; and whatsoever the mind of him that strongly hates, dictates, hath an efficacy to hurt and destroy. The like is in other things which the mind affects with a strong desire; for all those things which the mind acts, and dictates by *characters, figures, words, speeches, gestures, and the like*, help the appetite of the soul, and acquire certain wonderful virtues, from the soul of the operator, in that hour when such a like appetite doth invade it; so from the opportunity and celestial influence, moving the mind in this or that manner : for our mind, when it is carried upon the great excess of any passion or virtue, oftentimes takes to itself a strong, better and more convenient hour or opportunity; which Thomas Aquinas, in his third book against the Gentiles, allows. So, many wonderful virtues both cause and follow certain admirable operations by great affections, in those things which the soul doth dictate in that hour to them. But know, that such kind of things confer nothing, or very little, but to the author of them, and to him who is inclined to them, as if he were the author of them ; and this is the manner by which their efficacy is found out. And it is a general rule in them, that every mind, that is more excellent in its desire and affection, makes such like things more fit for itself, as also efficacious to that which it desires. Every one, therefore, that is willing to work in magic, must know the *virtue, measure, order*, and degree of his own soul in the power of the universe.

CHAP.

CHAP. XIV.

SHEWING THE NECESSITY OF MATHEMATICAL KNOWLEDGE, AND OF THE GREAT POWER
AND EFFICACY OF NUMBERS IN THE CONSTRUCTION OF TALISMANS, &c.

THE doctrines of mathematics are so necessary to and have such an affinity
with magic, that they who profess it without them are quite out of the way,
and labour in vain, and shall in no wise obtain their desired effect.   For whatsoever things are, and are done in these inferior natural virtues, are all done
and governed by *number, weight, measure, harmony, motion,* and *light:* and
all things which we see in these inferiors have root and foundation in them ;
yet, nevertheless, without natural virtues of mathematical doctrines, only
works like to naturals can be produced : as Plato saith---a thing not partaking
of truth or divinity, but certain images akin to them (as bodies going, or
speaking, which yet want the animal faculty), such as were those which,
amongst the ancients, were called Dedalus's images, and αυτοματα, of which
Aristotle makes mention, viz. the three-footed images of Vulcan and Dedalus
moving themselves ; which, Homer saith, came out of their own accord to the
exercise ; and which, we read, moved themselves at the feast of Hiarba, the
philosophical exerciser.   So there are made glasses (some concave, others of the
form of a column) making the representation of things in the air seem like
shadows at a distance ; of which sort Apollonius and Vitellius, in their books,
" De Prospectiva," and " Speculis," taught the making and the use.   And
we read that Magnus Pompeius brought a certain glass, amongst the spoils from
the East, to Rome, in which were seen armies of armed men.   And there are
made certain transparent glasses, which (being dipped in some certain juices of
herbs, and irradiated with an artificial light) fill the whole air round about
with visions.   And we know how to make reciprocal glasses, in which the sun
shining, all things which were illustrated by the rays thereof are apparently
seen many miles off.   Hence a magician (expert in natural philosophy and
mathematics, and knowing the middle sciences, consisting of both these, viz.
arithmetic, music, geometry, optics, astronomy, and such sciences that are of

weights,

weights, measures, proportions, articles, and joints ; knowing, also, mechanical arts resulting from these) may, without any wonder, if he excel other
men in the art and wit, do many wonderful things, which men may much
admire.　There are some relics now extant of the antients, viz. Hercules and
Alexander's pillars ; the gate of Caspia, made of brass, and shut with iron
beams, that it could by no art be broken ; and the pyramids of Julius Cæsar,
erected at Rome, near the hill Vaticanus; and mountains built by art in
the middle of the sea ; and towers, and heaps of stones, such as I have seen
in England, put together by incredible art.　But the vulgar seeing any wonderful sight, impute it to the Devil as his work; or think that a miracle
which, indeed, is a work of natural or mathematical philosophy.　But here it is
convenient that you know, that, as by natural virtues we collect natural virtues,
so by abstracted, mathematical, and celestial, we receive celestial virtues ; as
motion, sense, life, speech, soothsaying, and divination even in matter less disposed, as that which is not made by nature, but only by art.　And so images
that speak, and foretel things to come, are said to be made : as William of Paris
relates of a brazen-head, made under the rising of Saturn, which, they say,
spake with a man's voice.　But he that will chuse a disposed matter, and most
fit to receive, and a most powerful agent, shall undoubtedly produce more
powerful effects.　For it is a general opinion of the Pythagoreans, that, as
mathematical are more formal than natural, so also they are more efficacious ;
as they have less dependance in their being, so also in their operation.　But
amongst all mathematical things, *numbers*, as they have more of form in
them, so also are more efficacious, as well to affect what is good as what is
bad.　All things, which were first made by the nature of things in its first age,
seem to be formed by the proportion of numbers; for this was the principal
pattern in the mind of the Creator.　Hence is borrowed the number of the
elements---hence the courses of times---hence the motion of the stars, and the
revolution of the heavens, and the state of all things subsist by the uniting
together of numbers.　Numbers, therefore, are endowed with great and sublime virtues.　For it is no wonder, seeing there are so many occult virtues in
natural things, although of manifest operations, that there should be in numbers

bers much greater and more occult, and also more wonderful and efficacious ;
for as much as they are more formal, more perfect, and naturally in the celestials, not mixed with separated substances; and, lastly, having the greatest and
most simple commixion with the ideas in the mind of God, from which they
receive their proper and most efficacious virtues; wherefore they also are of
most force, and conduce most to the obtaining of spiritual and divine gifts---
as, in natural things, elementary qualities are powerful in the transmuting of
any elementary thing.   Again, all things that are, and are made, subsist by
and receive their virtue from numbers :---for time consists of numbers---and all
motion and action, and all things which are subject to time and motion.
Harmony, also, and voices have their power by and consist of numbers and
their proportions; and the proportion arising from numbers do, by lines and
points, make characters and figures; and these are proper to magical opera-
tions---the middle, which is betwixt both, being appropriated by declining to
the extremes, as in the use of letters.   And lastly, all species of natural things,
and of those which are above Nature, are joined together by certain numbers ;
which Pythagoras seeing, says, that number is that by which all things subsist, and distributes each virtue to each number.   And Proclus says, number
hath always a being : yet there is one in voice---another in proportion of
them---another in the soul and reason---and another in divine things.   But
Themistius, Boetius, and Averrois (the Babylonian), together with Plato, do
so extol numbers, that they think no man can be a true philosopher without
them.   By them there is a way made for the searching out and understanding of
all things knowable ;---by them the next access to natural prophecying is had
---and the Abbot Joachim proceeded no other way in his prophecies, but by
formal numbers.

CHAP.

CHAP. XV.

THE GREAT VIRTUES OF NUMBERS, AS WELL IN NATURAL THINGS AS IN SUPERNATURAL.

THAT there lies wonderful efficacy and virtue in numbers, as well to good as to bad, the most eminent philosophers unanimously teach ; especially Hierom, Austin, Origen, Ambrose, Gregory of Nazianzen, Athanasius, Basilius, Hilarius, Rubanas, Bede, and many more conform. Hence Hilarius, in his commentaries upon the Psalms, testifies that the seventy elders, according to the efficacy of numbers, brought the Psalms into order. The *natural number* is not here considered ; but the *formal* consideration that is in the number ;---and let that which we spoke before always be kept in mind, viz. that these powers are not in vocal numbers of merchants buying and selling ; but in rational, formal, and natural ;---these are the distinct mysteries of God and Nature. But he who knows how to join together the vocal numbers and natural with divine, and order them into the same harmony, shall be able to work and know wonderful things by numbers ; in which, unless there was a great mystery, John had not said, in the Revelation---" He that hath understanding, let him compute the number of the name of the beast, which is the number of a man ;"---and this is the most famous manner of computing amongst the Hebrews and Cabalists, as we shall shew afterwards. But this you must know, that simple numbers signify divine things, numbers of ten ; celestial numbers of an hundred ; terrestrial numbers of a thousand---those things that shall be in a future age. Besides, seeing the parts of the mind are according to an arithmetical mediocrity, by reason of the identity, or equality of excess, coupled together ; but the body, whose parts differ in their greatness, is, according to a geometrical mediocrity, compounded ; but an animal consists of both, viz. soul and body, according to that mediocrity which is. suitable to harmony. Hence it is that *numbers* work very much upon the *soul*, *figures* upon the *body*, and *harmony* upon the *whole animal*.

CHAP.

CHAP. XVI.
OF THE SCALE OF UNITY.

NOW let us treat particularly of numbers themselves; and, because number is nothing else but a repetition of unity, let us first consider unity itself; for unity doth most simply go through every number, and is the common measure, fountain, and original of all numbers; contains every number joined together in itself entirely; the beginner of every multitude, always the same, and unchangeable; whence, also, being multiplied into itself, produceth nothing but itself: it is indivisible, void of all parts. Nothing is before one, nothing is after one, and beyond it is nothing; and all things which are, desire that one, because all things proceed from one; and that all things may be the same, it is necessary that they partake of that one: and as all things proceed of one into many things, so all things endeavour to return to that one, from which they proceeded; it is necessary that they should put off multitude. One, therefore, is referred to the most high God, who, seeing he is one and innumerable, yet creates innumerable things of himself, and contains them within himself. There is, therefore, one God---one world of the one God--- one sun of the one world---also one phœnix in the world---one king amongst bees---one leader amongst flocks of cattle---one ruler amongst herds of beasts--- and cranes follow one, and many other animals honour unity. Amongst the members of the body there is one principal, by which all the rest are guided; whether it be the head, or (as some will) the heart. There is one element, overcoming and penetrating all things, viz. fire. There is one thing created of God, the subject of *all wondering* which is in earth or in heaven---it is actually animal, vegetable, and mineral; every where found, known by few, called by none by its proper name, but covered with figures and riddles, without which neither Alchymy, nor Natural Magic can attain to their complete end or perfection. From one man, Adam, all men proceeded---from that one, all became mortal---from that one, *Jesus Christ*, they are regenerated; and, as saith St. Paul, one Lord, one faith, one baptism, one God and Father of all, one

Mediator

Mediator betwixt God and man, one most high Creator, who is over all, by all, and in us all, For there is one Father, God, from whence all, and we in him; one Lord Jesus Christ, by whom all, and we by him; one God Holy Ghost, into whom all, and we into him.

THE SCALE OF UNITY.

In the Exemplary World,	Jod.	One Divine Essence, the fountain of all virtues and power, whose name is expressed with one most simple letter.
In the Intellectual World,	The Soul of the World.	One Supreme Intelligence, the first creature, the fountain of life.
In the Celestial World,	The Sun.	One King of Stars, the fountain of life.
In the Elemental World,	The Philosophers' Stone.	One subject, and instrument of all virtues, natural and supernatural.
In the Lesser World,	The Heart.	One first living and last dying.
In the Infernal World,	Lucifer.	One Prince of Rebellion, of Angels, and Darkness.

CHAP. XVII.

OF THE NUMBER TWO, AND SCALE.

THE first number is two, because it is the first multitude; it can be measured by no number besides unity alone, the common measure of all numbers; it is not compounded of numbers, but of one unity only; neither is it called a number uncompounded, but more properly not compounded. The number three, is called the first number uncompounded. But the number two is the first branch of unity, and the first procreation; and it is called the number of science, and memory, and of light, and the number of man, who is called

another

another, and the lesser world : it is also called the number of charity, and of
mutual love ; of marriage, and society : as it is said by the Lord---" Two shall
be one flesh."---And Solomon saith, " It is better that two be together than one,
for they have a benefit by their mutual society : if one shall fall, he shall be
supported by the other. Woe to him that is alone ; because, when he falls, he
hath not another to help him. And if two sleep together, they shall warm one
another ; how shall one be hot alone ?---And if any prevail against him, two
resist him." And it is called the number of wedlock, and sex ; for there are
two sexes---masculine and feminine. And two doves bring forth two eggs ;
out of the first of which is hatched the male, out of the second the female. It
is also called the middle, that is capable, that is good and bad, partaking ;
and the beginning of division, of multitude, and distinction ; and signifies matter. This is also, sometimes, the number of discord, of confusion, of misfortune, and uncleanness ; whence St. Hierom, against Jovianus, saith---" that
therefore it was not spoken in the second day of the creation of the world."---
" And God said, that it was good ;"---because the number of two is evil.
Hence also it was, that God commanded that all unclean animals should go
into the ark by couples ; because, as I said, the number of two is a number of
uncleanness. Pythagorus, as Eusebius reports, said, that unity was God, and
a good intellect ; but that duality was a devil, and an evil intellect, in which
is a material multitude : wherefore the Pythagorians say, that two is not a
number, but a certain confusion of unities. And Plutarch writes, that the
Pythagorians called unity, Apollo ; and two, strife and boldness ; and three,
justice, which is the highest perfection, and is not without many mysteries.
Hence there were two tables of the law in Sinai---two cherubims looking to
the propitiatory in Moses---two olives dropping oil, in Zachariah---two natures
in Christ, divine and human : hence Moses saw two appearances of God, viz.
his face, and back parts ;---also two Testaments---two commands of love---two
first dignities---two first people---two kinds of spirits, good and bad---two intellectual creatures, an angel and soul---two great lights---two solstitia---two
equinoctials---two poles---two elements, producing a living soul, viz. earth
and water.

Book I.   THE

THE SCALE OF THE NUMBER TWO.

In the Exemplary World,	יה Jah אל El		The names of God, expressed with two Letters.
In the Intellectual World,	An Angel,	The Soul;	Two Intelligible Substances.
In the Celestial World,	The Sun,	The Moon;	Two great Lights.
In the Elementary World,	The Earth,	The Water;	Two Elements producing a living Soul.
In the Lesser World,	The Heart,	The Brain;	Two principal Seats of the Soul.
In the Infernal World,	Beemoth, weeping,	Leviathan, gnashing of teeth;	Two Chiefs of the Devils. Two things Christ threatens to the damned.

CHAP. XVIII.

OF THE NUMBER THREE AND SCALE.

THE number Three, is an uncompounded number, a holy number, a number of perfection, a most powerful number :---for there are three persons in God ; there are three theological virtues in religion.   Hence it is that this number conduceth to the ceremonies of God and religion, that by the solemnity of which, prayers and sacrifices are thrice repeated ; for corporeal and spiritual things consist of three things, viz. beginning, middle, and end. By three, as Trismegistus saith, the world is perfected---harmony, necessity, and order, i. e. concurrence of causes (which many call fate), and the execution of them to the fruit, or increase, or a due distribution of the increase. The whole measure of time is concluded in three, viz. past, present, and to come ;---all magnitude is contained in three---line, superfices, and body ;---

every

every body consists of three intervals,---length, breadth, and thickness.   Harmony contains three consents in time---diapason, hemiolion, diatesseron. There are also three kinds of souls---vegetative, sensitive, and intellectual. And as such, saith the Prophet, God orders the world by number, weight, and measure; and the number three is deputed to the ideal forms thereof, as the number two is the procreating matter, and unity to God the maker of it.---Magicians do constitute three Princes of the world---Oromasis, Mithris, Araminis; *i. e.* God, the mind, and the spirit.   By the three-square or solid, the three numbers of nine, of things produced, are distributed, viz. of the supercelestial into nine orders of intelligences ; of celestial, into nine orbs ; of inferiors, into nine kinds of generable and corruptible things.   Lastly, into this eternal orb, viz. twenty-seven, all musical proportions are included, as Plato and Proclus do at large discourse ; and the number three hath, in a harmony of five, the grace of the first voice.   Also, in intelligences, there are three hierarchies of angelical spirits.   There are three powers of intellectual creatures---memory, mind, and will.   There are three orders of the blessed, viz. martyrs, confessors, and innocents.   There are three quaternions of celestial signs, viz. of fixed, moveable, and common ; as also of houses, viz. centres, succeeding, and falling.   There are, also, three faces and heads in every sign, and three Lords of each triplicity.   There are three fortunes amongst the planets.   In the infernal crew, three judges, three furies, three-headed Cerberus : we read, also, of a thrice-double Hecate.   Three months of the Virgin Diana.   Three persons in the super-substantial Divinity.   Three times---of nature, law, and grace.   Three theological virtues---faith, hope, and charity.   Jonah was three days in the whale's belly ; and so many was Christ in the grave.

THE

THE SCALE OF THE NUMBER THREE.

In the Original World,	The Father,	Adai, The Son,	The Holy Ghost ;	The Name of God with three Letters.
In the Intellectual World,	Supreme Innocents,	Middle Martyrs,	Lowest of all Confessors ;	Three hierarchies of Angels. Three degrees of the Blessed.
In the Celestial World,	Moveable, Corners, Of the Day,	Fixed, Succeeding, Nocturnal,	Common ; Falling ; Partaking ;	Three quaternions of Signs. Three quaternions of houses. Three Lords of triplicities.
In the Elementary World,	Simple,	Compounded,	Thrice compounded ;	Three degrees of elements.
In the Lesser World,	The head, in which the intellect grows, answering to the intellectual world,	The breast, where is the heart, the seat of life, answering to the celestial world,	The belly, where the faculty of generation is, and the genital members, answering the elemental world ;	Three parts, answering to the threefold world.
In the Infernal World,	Alecto, Minos, Wicked,	Megera, Acacus, Apostates,	Ctesiphone ; Rhadamantus ; Infidels ;	Three infernal Furies. Three infernal Judges. Three degrees of the damned.

CHAP. XIX.

OF THE NUMBER FOUR AND SCALE.

THE Pythagorians call the number Four, Tectractis, and prefer it before all the virtues of numbers, because it is the foundation and root of all other numbers; whence, also, all foundations, as well in artificial things, as natural and divine, are four square, as we shall shew afterwards ; and it signifies solidity, which also is demonstrated by a four-square figure ; for the number four, is the first

four-

four-square plane, which consists of two proportions, whereof the first is of one to two, the latter of two to four; and it proceeds by a double procession and proportion, viz. of one to one, and of two to two---beginning at a unity, and ending at a quaternity: which proportions differ in this, that, according to Arithmetic, they are unequal to one another, but according to Geometry, are equal. Therefore a four-square is ascribed to God the Father; and also contains the mystery of the whole Trinity: for by its single proportion, viz. by the first of one to one, the unity of the paternal substance is signified, from which proceeds one Son, equal to Him;---by the next procession, also simple, viz. of two to two, is signified (by the second procession) the Holy Ghost; from both---that the Son be equal to the Father, by the first procession; and the Holy Ghost be equal to both, by the second procession. Hence that superexcellent and great name of the Divine Trinity in God is written with four letters, viz. *Jod, He,* and *Van.* He, where it is the aspiration He, signifies the proceeding of the Spirit from both; for He, being duplicated, terminates both syllables, and the whole name, but is pronounced Jova, as some will whence that Jove of the heathen, which the antients did picture with four ears; whence the number four, is the fountain and head of the whole, Divinity. And the Pythagorians call it the perpetual fountain of Nature: for there are four degrees in the scale of Nature, viz. *to be, to live, to be sensible, to understand.* There are four motions in Nature, viz. ascendant, descendant, going forward, circular. There are four corners in Heaven, viz. rising, falling, the middle of the Heaven, the bottom of it. There are four elements under Heaven, viz. fire, air, water, and earth; according to these there are four triplicities in Heaven. There are four first qualities under Heaven, viz. cold, heat, dryness, and moisture; from these are the four humours---blood, phlegm, choler, melancholy. Also, the year is divided into four parts, which are the spring, summer, autumn, and winter:---also the wind is divided into eastern, western, northern, and southern. There are, also, four rivers in Paradise; and so many infernal. Also, the number four makes

up

up all knowledge : first, it fills up every simple progress of numbers with four terms, viz. with one, two, three, and four, constituting the number ten. It fills up every difference of numbers : the first even, and containing the first odd in it. It hath in music, diatesseron---the grace of the fourth voice; also it contains the instrument of four strings; and a Pythagorian diagram, whereby are found out first of all musical tunes, and all harmony of music : for double, treble, four times double, one and a half, one and a third part, a concord of all, a double concord of all, of five, of four, and all consonancy is limited within the bounds of the number four. It doth also contain the whole of Mathematics in four terms, viz. *point, line, superfices*, and *profundity*. It comprehends all Nature in four terms, viz. substance, quality, quantity, and motion; also all natural philosophy, in which are the seminary virtues of Nature, the natural springing, the growing form, and the *compositum*. Also metaphysics is comprehended in four bounds, viz. *being, essence, virtue*, and *action*. Moral philosophy is comprehended with four virtues, viz. *prudence, justice, fortitude*, and *temperance*. It hath also the power of justice : hence a four-fold law---of *providence*, from God ; *fatal*, from the soul of the world; of *Nature*, from Heaven ; of *prudence*, from man. There are also four judiciary powers in all things being, viz. the intellect, discipline, opinion, and sense. Also, there are four rivers of Paradise. Four Gospels, received from four Evangelists, throughout the whole Church. The Hebrews received the chiefest name of God written with four letters. Also the Egyptians, Arabians, Persians, Magicians, Mahometans, Grecians, Tuscans, and Latins, write the name of God with four letters, viz. thus---Thet, Alla, Sire, Orsi, Abdi, θεὸς, Esar, Deus. Hence the Lacedemonians were wont to paint Jupiter with four wings. Hence, also, in Orpheus's Divinity, it is said that Neptune's chariots are drawn with four horses. There are also four kinds of divine furies proceeding from several deities, viz. from the Muses, Dionysius, Apollo, and Venus. Also, the Prophet Ezekiel saw four beasts by the river Chobar, and four cherubims in four wheels. Also, in Daniel, four great beasts did ascend

from

from the sea; and four winds did fight. And in the Revelations, four beasts were full of eyes, before and behind, standing round about the throne of God; and for angels, to whom was given power to hurt the earth and the sea, did stand upon the four corners of the earth, holding the four winds, that they should not blow upon the earth, nor upon the sea, nor upon any tree.

THE

THE SCALE OF

The name of God with four letters,	יהוה				In the original world, whence the law of Providence.
Four triplicities, or intelligible hierarchies,	Seraphim, Cherubim, Thrones,	Dominations, Powers, Virtues,	Principalities, Archangels, Angels,	Innocents, Martyrs, Confessors.	In the intellectual world, whence the fatal law.
Four angels ruling over the four corners of the world,	מיכאל Michael,	רפאל Raphael,	גבריאל Gabriel,	אוריאל Uriel.	
Four rulers of the elements,	שרפ Seraph,	כרוב Cherub,	תרשיט Tharsis,	אריאל Ariel.	
Four consecrated animals,	The Lion,	The Eagle,	. Man, .	A Calf.	
Four triplicities of the tribes of Israel,	Dan, Asser, Naphthalin,	Jehuda, Isachar, Zebulun,	Manasse, Benjamin, Ephraim,	Reuben, Simeon, Gad.	
Four triplicities of the Apostles,	Matthias, Peter, Jacob the elder,	Simon, Bartholomew, Matthew,	John, Philip, James the younger	Thaddeus, Andrew, Thomas.	
Four Evangelists,	Mark,	John,	Matthew,	Luke.	
Four triplicities of signs,	Aries, Leo, Sagittarius,	Gemini, Libra, Aquarius,	Cancer, Scorpion, Pisces,	Taurus, Virgo, Capricornus.	In the celestial world, where is the law of Nature.
The stars and planets related to the elements,	Mars, and the Sun,	Jupiter, and Venus,	Saturn, and Mercury,	The fixed Stars, and the Moon.	
Four qualities of the celestial elements,	Light,	Diaphanousness,	Agility,	Solidity.	
Four elements,	אש Fire,	ריח Air,	כוים Water,	עפר Earth.	In the elementary, where the law of generation and corruption is.
Four qualities,	Heat,	Moisture,	Cold,	Dryness.	
Four seasons,	Summer,	Spring,	Winter,	Autumn.	
Four corners of the world,	East,	West,	North,	South.	
Four perfect kinds of mixed bodies,	Animals,	Plants,	Metals,	Stones.	
Four kinds of animals,	Walking,	Flying,	Swimming,	Creeping.	

THE NUMBER FOUR.

What answers the elements in plants,	Seeds,	Flowers,	Leaves,	Roots.
What in metals,	Gold and iron,	Copper and tin,	Quicksilver,	Lead and silver.
What in stones,	Bright and burning,	Light and transparent,	Clear and congealed,	Heavy and dark.
Four elements of man,	The Mind,	Spirit,	Soul,	Body.
Four powers of the soul,	The Intellect,	Reason,	Phantasy,	Sense.
Four judiciary powers,	Faith,	Science,	Opinion,	Experience.
Four moral virtues,	Justice,	Temperance,	Prudence,	Fortitude.
The senses answering to the elements,	Sight,	Hearing,	Taste and smell,	Touch.
Four elements of man's body,	Spirit,	Flesh,	Humours,	Bones.
A fourfold spirit,	Animal,	Vital,	Generative,	Natural.
Four humours,	Choler,	Blood,	Phlegm,	Melancholy.
Four manners of complexion,	Violence,	Nimbleness,	Dulness,	Slowness.
Four princes of devils, offensive in the elements,	סמאל Samael,	עזאזל Azazel,	עזאל Azael,	מהזאל Mahazael.
Four infernal rivers,	Phlegethon,	Cocytus,	Styx,	Acheron.
Four princes of spirits, upon the four angles of the world,	Oriens,	Paymon,	Egyn,	Amaymon.

In the lesser world, viz. man, from whom is the law of prudence.

In the infernal world, where is the law of wrath and punishment.

CHAP. XX.

OF THE NUMBER FIVE, AND ITS SCALE.

THE number Five is of no small force; for it consists of the first even and the first odd; as of a female and male : for an odd number is the male, and the even the female; whence arithmeticians call that the father, and this the mother. Therefore the number five is of no small perfection or virtue, which proceeds from the mixtion of these numbers; it is, also, the just middle of the universal number, viz. ten : for if you divide the number ten, there will be nine and one, or eight and two, and seven and three, or six and four, and every collection makes the number ten, and the exact middle is always the number five, and its equa-distant; and therefore it is called, by the Pythagorians, the number of wedlock, as also of justice, because it divides the number ten in an even scale. There are five senses in man---sight, hearing, smelling, tasting, and feeling; five powers in the soul---vegetative, sensitive, concupiscible, irascible, and rational; five fingers on the hand; five wandering planets in the heavens, according to which there are fivefold terms in every sign. In elements there are five kinds of mixed bodies, viz. stones, metals, plants, plant-animals, animals; and so many kinds of animals---as men, four-footed beasts, creeping, swimming, and flying. And there are five kinds by which all things are made of God, viz. essence, the same, another, sense, and motion. The swallow brings forth but five young, which she feeds with equity, beginning with the eldest, and so the rest according to their age. For in this number the father Noah found favour with God, and was preserved in the flood of waters. In the virtue of this number, Abraham, being an hundred years old, begat a son of Sarah (Sarah being ninety years old, and a barren woman, and past childbearing), and grew up to be a great people. Hence, in time of grace, the name of Divine Omnipotency is called upon in five letters; in time of nature, the name of God was called upon with three letters שדי Sadai; in time of the law, the ineffable name of God was expressed with four letters יהוה, instead of which the Hebrews express אדני Adonai; in time of grace, the ineffable

name

name of God was written with five letters יהשוה Jhesu, which is called upon with no less mystery than that of three letters שׁי.

THE SCALE OF THE NUMBER FIVE.

The Names of God with five letters. The Name of Christ with five letters,		אליון אלהים יהשוה	Eloim, Elohi, Jhesu,			In the exemplary world.
Five intelligible substances,	Spirits of the first hierarchy, called Gods, or the sons of God,	Spirits of the second hierarchy, called Intelligences,	Spirits of the third hierarchy, called Angels which are sent,	Souls of celestial bodies,	Heroes and blessed souls.	In the intellectual world.
Five wandering stars, lords of the terms,	Saturn,	Jupiter,	Mars,	Venus,	Mercury.	In the celestial world.
Five kinds of corruptible things,	Water,	Air,	Fire,	Earth,	A mixed body.	In the elementary world.
Five kinds of mixed bodies,	Animal,	Plant,	Metal,	Stone,	Plant-animal.	
Five senses,	Taste,	Hearing,	Seeing,	Touching,	Smelling.	In the lesser world.
Five corporeal torments,	Deadly bitterness,	Horrible howling,	Terrible darkness,	Unquenchable heat,	A piercing stink.	In the infernal world.

CHAP. XXI.

OF THE NUMBER SIX, AND THE SCALE.

SIX is a number of perfection, because it is the most perfect in nature, in the whole course of numbers, from one to ten; and it alone is so perfect that in the collection of its parts, it results the same, neither wanting nor abounding

ing

ing; for if the parts thereof, viz. the middle, third, and sixth part, which are three, two, one, be gathered together, they perfectly fill up the whole body of six, which perfection all the other numbers want. Hence, by the Pythagorians, it is said to be altogether to be applied to generation and marriage, and is called the scale of the world; for the world is made of the number six---neither doth it abound, nor is defective: hence that is, because the world was finished by God the sixth day; for the sixth day God saw all things which he had made, and they were * *very good;* therefore the heaven, and the earth, and all the host thereof, were finished. It is also called the number of man, because the sixth day † man was created. And it is also the number of our redemption; for on the sixth day Christ suffered for our redemption; whence there is a great affinity between the number six and the cross, labour, and servitude. Hence it is commanded in the law, that in six days the manna is to be gathered, and work to be done. Six years the ground was to be sown; and that the Hebrew servant was to serve his master six years. Six days the glory of the Lord appeared upon Mount Sinai, covering it with a cloud. The Cherubims had six wings. Six circles in the firmament: Artic, Antartic, two Tropics, Equinoctial and Ecliptical. Six wandering planets: Saturn, Jupiter, Mars, Venus, Mercury, the Moon, running through the latitude of the Zodiac on both sides the Ecliptic. There are six substantial qualities in the elements, viz. sharpness, thinness, motion; and the contrary to these---dulness, thickness, and rest. There are six differences of position: upwards, downwards, before, behind, on the right side, and on the left side. There are six natural offices, without which nothing can be, viz. magnitude, colour, figure, interval, standing, motion. Also, a solid figure of any four-square thing hath six superfices. There are six tones of all harmony, viz. five tones, and two half tones which make one tone, which is the sixth.

---

* The sixth day, the Eternal Wisdom pronounced all things created by his divine hand to be " *very good.*"

† Hence arose the mystery of the number of the beast, six hundred three score and six, being the number of a man---DCLXVI.

SCALE

THE SCALE OF THE NUMBER SIX.

In the Exemplary World,	אל גבוראלוהים						Names of six letters.
In the Intelligible World,	Seraphim,	Cherubim,	Thrones,	Domina-tions,	Powers,	Virtues ;	Six orders of Angels, which are not sent to inferiors.
In the Celestial World.	Saturn,	Jupiter,	Mars,	Venus,	Mercury,	The Moon ;	Six planets wandering through the latitude of the Zodiac from the Ecliptic.
In the Elemental World,	Rest,	Thinness,	Sharpness,	Dulness,	Thickness,	Motion ;	Six substantial qualities of the elements.
In the Lesser World,	The Intellect,	Memory,	Sense,	Motion,	Life,	Essence ;	Six degrees of the mind.
In the Infernal World,	Acteus,	Megalesius,	Ormenus,	Lycus,	Nicon,	Mimon ;	Six Devils, the authors of all calamities.

CHAP. XXII.

OF THE NUMBER SEVEN, AND THE SCALE.

THE number Seven is of various and manifold power; for it consists of one and six, or of two and five, or of three and four; and it hath a unity, as it were the coupling together of two threes : whence if we consider the several parts thereof, and the joining together of them, without doubt we shall confess that it is, as well by the joining together of the parts thereof as by its fulness apart, most full of all majesty. And the Pythagorians call it the *vehiculum* of man's life, which it doth not receive from its parts so, as it perfects by its

proper

proper right of its whole---for it contains body and soul; for the body consists
of four elements, and is endowed with four qualities : also, the number three
respects the soul, by reason of its threefold power, viz. rational, irascible, and
concupiscible.   The number seven, therefore, because it consists of three and
four, joins the soul to the body; and the virtue of this number relates to the
generation of men, and it causes man to be received, formed, brought forth,
nourished, live, and indeed altogether to subsist : for when the genital seed is
received in the womb of the woman, if it remains there seven hours after the
effusion of it, it is certain that it will abide there for good; then the first seven
days it is coagulated, and is fit to receive the shape of a man; then it pro-
duces mature infants, which are called infants of the seventh month, *i. e.* because they are born the seventh month; after the birth, the seventh hour tries
whether it will live or no---for that which will bear the breath of the air after
that hour, is conceived will live; after seven days, it casts off the relics of the
navel; after twice seven days, its sight begins to move after the light; in the
third seventh, it turns its eyes and whole face freely; after seven months, it
breeds teeth; after the second seventh month, it sits without fear of falling;
after the third seventh month, it begins to speak; after the fourth seventh
month, it stands strongly and walks; after the fifth seventh month, it begins
to refrain sucking its nurse; after seven years, its first teeth fall, and new are
bred, fitter for harder meat, and its speech is perfected; after the second
seventh year, boys wax ripe, and then it is a beginning of generation at the
third seventh year, they grow to men in stature, and begin to be hairy, and
become able and strong for generation; at the fourth seventh year, they cease
to grow taller; in the fifth seventh year, they attain to the perfection of their
strength; the sixth seventh year, they keep their strength; the seventh seventh
year, they attain to their utmost discretion and wisdom, and the perfect age of
men; but when they come to the tenth seventh year, where the number seven
is taken for a complete number, then they come to the common term of life---
the Prophet saying, our age is seventy years.   The utmost height of a man's
body is seven feet.   There are, also, seven degrees in the body, which complete the dimension of its altitude from the bottom to the top, viz. marrow,
bone, nerve, vein, artery, flesh, and skin.   There are seven, which, by the
                                                                          Greeks

Greeks, are called black members : the tongue, heart, lungs, liver, spleen, and the two kidnies.   There are, also, seven principal parts, of the body : the head, breast, hands, feet, and the privy members.   It is manifest, concerning breath and meat, that, without drawing of the breath, the life doth not remain above seven hours ; and they that are starved with famine, live not above seven days.*   The veins, also, and arteries, as physicians say, are moved by the seventh number.   Also, judgments in diseases are made with greater manifestation upon the seventh day, which physicians call critical, *i. e.* judicial.   Also, of seven portions God creates the soul ;---the soul, also, receives the body by seven degrees.   All difference of voices proceeds to the seventh degree, after which there is the same revolution.   Again, there are seven modulations of the voices : ditonus, semiditonus, diatesseron, diapente with a tone, diapente with a half tone, and diapason.   There are also, in celestials, a most potent power of the number seven ; for seeing there are four corners of the Heaven diametrically looking one towards the other, which indeed is accounted a most full and powerful aspect, and consists of the number seven ; for it is made with the seventh sign, and makes a cross, the most powerful figure of all, of which we shall speak in its due place ;---but this you must not be ignorant of, that the number seven hath a great communion with the cross.   By the same radiation and number the solstice is distant from winter, and the winter equinoctium from the summer, all which are done by seven signs.   There are also seven circles in the Heavens, according to the longitudes of the axle-tree. There are seven stars about the Arctic Pole, greater and lesser, called Charles Wain ; also seven stars called the Pleiades ; and seven planets, according to those seven days constituting a week.   The Moon is the seventh of the planets, and next to us, observing this number more than the rest, this number dispensing the motion and light thereof ; for in twenty-eight days, it runs round the compass of the whole Zodiac ; which number of days, the number seven with its seven terms, viz. from one to seven, doth make and fill up as much as the

---

* There have been some exceptions to this affirmation, one of which fell under my notice of late years: Doctor Edward Spry, of Plymouth Dock, Philosopher, Cabalist, and Physician, lived upwards of two years upon a gooseberry a day in summer, and an oat cake and three glasses of white wine the rest of the season, per day : this gentleman was particularly abstemious in his diet.

several

several numbers, by adding to the antecedents, and makes four times seven days, in which the Moon runs through and about all the longitude and latitude of the Zodiac, by measuring and measuring again : with the like seven days it dispenses its light, by changing it; for the first seven days, unto the middle as it were of the divided world, it increases; the second seven days it fills its whole orb with light; the third, by decreasing, is again contracted into a divided orb; but, after the fourth seven days, it is renewed with the last diminution of its light; and by the same seven days, it disposes the increase and decrease of the sea : for in the first seven of the increase of the moon, it is by little and little lessened; in the second, by degrees increased; but the third is like the first, and the fourth does the same as the second. It is also applied to Saturn, which ascending from the lower, is the seventh planet, which betokens rest; to which the seventh day is ascribed, which signifies the seven thousandth, wherein, as St. John says, the dragon (which is the devil) and satan being bound, men shall be quiet, and lead a peaceable life. And the leprous person that was to be cleansed, was sprinkled seven times with the blood of a sparrow; and Elisha the Prophet, as it is written in the second book of Kings, saith unto the leprous person---" Go, and wash thyself seven times in Jordan, and thy flesh shall be made whole, and thou shalt be cleansed."--- Also, it is a number of repentance and remission. And Christ, with seven petitions, finished his speech of our satisfaction. It is called the number of liberty, because the seventh year the Hebrew servant did challenge liberty for himself. It is also most suitable to divine praises; whence the Prophet saith--- " Seven times a day do I praise thee, because of thy righteous judgments."--- It is moreover called the number of revenge, as says the Scripture---" And Cain shall be revenged sevenfold."---And the Psalmist says---" Render unto our neighbours sevenfold into their bosom their reproach."---Hence there are seven wickednesses, as saith Solomon; and seven wickeder spirits taken, are read of in the Gospel. It signifies, also, the time of the present circle, because it is finished in the space of seven days. Also it is consecrated to the Holy Ghost; which the Prophet Isaiah describes to be sevenfold, according to his gift, viz. the spirit of wisdom and understanding, the spirit of counsel and strength, the spirit of knowledge and holiness, the spirit of fear of the Lord,

which

which we read in Zachariah to be the *seven eyes of God*. There are also seven angels, spirits standing in the presence of God, as is read in Tobias, and in the Revelation : seven lamps did burn before the throne of God, and seven golden candlesticks, and in the middle thereof was one like unto the Son of Man, and he had in his right hand seven stars. Also, there were seven spirits before the throne of God, and seven angels stood before the throne, and there were given to them seven trumpets. And he saw a Lamb, having seven horns and seven eyes ; and he saw the book sealed with seven seals ; and when the seventh seal was opened, there was made silence in Heaven.

Now, by all that has been said, it is apparent that the number seven, amongst the other numbers, may be deservedly said to be most full of efficacy. Moreover, the number seven hath great conformity with the number twelve ; for as three and four make seven, so thrice four makes twelve, which are the numbers of the celestial planets and signs resulting from the same root ; and by the number three partaking of the Divinity, and by the number four of the nature of inferior things. There is in sacred writ a very great observance of this number before all others, and many, and very great are the mysteries thereof : many we have decreed to reckon up here, repeating them out of holy writ, by which it will easily appear that the number seven doth signify a certain fulness of sacred mysteries ; for we read, in Genesis, that the seventh was the day of rest of the Lord ; that Enoch, a pious holy man, was the seventh from Adam ; and that there was another seventh man from Adam, a wicked man, by name Lamech, that had two wives ; and that the sin of Cain should be abolished the seventh generation, as it is written---Cain shall be punished sevenfold ; and that he who shall slay Cain, shall be revenged sevenfold ; to which the master of the history collects that there were seven sins of Cain. Also, of all clean beasts seven, and seven were brought into the ark, as also of fowls ; and after seven days the Lord rained upon the earth ; and upon the seventh day the fountains of the deep were broken up, and the waters covered the earth. Also, Abraham gave to Abimelech seven ewe lambs ; and Jacob served seven years for Leah, and seven more for Rachel ; and seven days the people of Israel bewailed the death of Jacob.   Moreover we read, in the same place, of seven kine; and seven years of corn ; seven years of plenty, and seven years of scarcity.   And in Exodus, the Sabbath of Sabbaths, the holy rest to the Lord, is commanded to be on the seventh day ; also, on the seventh day Moses ceased to pray.   On the seventh day there shall be a solemnity of the Lord; the seventh year the servant shall go out free ; seven days let the calf and the lamb be with its dam; the seventh year, let the ground that hath been sown six years be at rest; the seventh day shall be a holy Sabbath, and a rest; the seventh day, because it is the Sabbath, shall be called holy.   In Leviticus, the seventh day also shall be more observed, and be more holy ; and the first day of the seventh month shall be a Sabbath of memorial ; seven days shall the sacrifices be offered to the Lord ; seven days shall the holy days of the Lord be celebrated ; seven days in a year everlastingly in the generations.   In the seventh month you shall celebrate feasts, and shall dwell in tabernacles seven days ; seven times he shall sprinkle himself before the Lord that hath dipped his finger in blood ; he that is cleansed from the leprosy, shall dip seven times in the blood of a sparrow ; seven days shall she be washed with running water that is menstruous ; seven times he shall dip his finger in the blood of a bullock ; seven times I will smite you for your sins.   In Deuteronomy, seven people possessed the Land of Promise.   There is also read, a seventh year of remission ; and seven candles set up on the south side of the candlesticks. And in Numbers it is read, that the sons of Israel offered up seven ewe lambs without spot ; and that seven days they did eat unleavened bread ; and that sin was expiated with seven lambs and a goat ; and that the seventh day was celebrated, and holy ; and the first day of the seventh month was observed, and kept holy ; and the seventh month of the Feast of Tabernacles ; and seven calves were offered on the seventh day ; and Baalam erected seven altars ; seven days Mary, the sister of Aaron, went forth leprous out of the camp ; seven days he that touched a dead carcass was unclean.   And in Joshua, seven priests carried the ark of the covenant before the host ; and seven days they

went

went round the cities; and seven trumpets were carried by the seven priests; and on the seventh day, the seven priests sounded the trumpets. And in the book of Judges, Abessa reigned in Israel seven years; Sampson kept his nuptials seven days, and the seventh day he put forth a riddle to his wife; he was bound with seven green withes; seven locks of his head were shaved off; seven years were the children of Israel oppressed by the King of Maden. And in the books of the Kings, Elias prayed seven times, and at the seventh time beheld a little cloud; seven days the children of Israel pitched over against the Syrians, and in the seventh day of the battle were joined: seven years' famine was threatened to David, for the people's murmuring; and seven times the child sneezed that was raised by Elisha; and seven men were crucified together, in the days of the first harvest; Naaman was made clean with seven washings, by Elisha; the seventh month Goliah was slain. And in Hester we read, that the King of Persia had seven eunuchs. And in Tobias, seven men were coupled with Sarah, the daughter of Raguel. And, in Daniel, Nebuchadnezzar's furnace was heated seven times hotter than it was used to be; and seven lions were in the den, and the seventh day came Nebuchadnezzar. In the book of Job, there is mention of seven sons of Job; and seven days and nights Job's friends sat with him on the earth; and, in the same place---"In seven troubles no evil shall come near thee." In Ezra, we read of Artaxerxes's seven counsellors; and in the same place, the trumpet sounded; the seventh month of the Feast of Tabernacles was, in Ezra's time, whilst the children of Israel were in the cities; and on the first day of the seventh month, Esdras read the law to the people. And in the Psalms, David praised the Lord seven times in the day; silver is tried seven times; and he renders to his neighbours sevenfold into their bosoms. And Solomon saith, that Wisdom hath hewn herself seven pillars; seven men that can render a reason; seven abominations which the Lord abhors; seven abominations in the heart of an enemy; seven overseers; seven eyes beholding. Isaiah numbers up seven gifts of the Holy Ghost; and seven women shall take hold on a man. And in Jeremiah, if she that hath

borne

borne seven, languishes, she has given up the ghost. In Ezekiel, the Prophet continued sad for seven days. In Zachariah, seven lamps, and seven pipes to those seven lamps; and seven eyes running to and fro through the whole earth; and seven eyes on one stone; and the fast of the seventh day is turned into joy. And in Micah, seven shepherds are raised against the Assyrians. Also, in the Gospel, we read of seven blessings; and seven virtues, to which seven vices are opposed; seven petitions of the Lord's Prayer; seven words of Christ upon the cross; seven words of the blessed Virgin Mary; seven loaves distributed by the Lord; seven baskets of fragments; seven brothers having one wife; seven disciples of the Lord who were fishers; seven water pots in Cana of Galilee; seven woes which the Lord threatens to hypocrites; seven devils cast out of the unclean woman, and seven wickeder devils taken in after that which was cast out; also, seven years Christ was fled into Egypt; and the seventh hour the fever left the governor's son. And in the canonical epistles, James describes seven degrees of wisdom; and Peter, seven degrees of virtues. And in the Acts, we reckon seven deacons, and seven disciples chosen by the Apostles. Also, in the Revelation, there are many mysteries relating to this number; for there we read of seven candlesticks, seven stars, seven crowns, seven churches, seven spirits before the throne, seven rivers of Egypt, seven seals, seven marks, seven horns, seven eyes, seven spirits of God, seven angels with seven trumpets, seven horns of the dragon, seven heads of the dragon which had seven diadems, also seven plagues, and seven vials which were given to every one of the seven angels, seven heads of the scarlet beast, seven mountains and seven kings sitting upon them, and seven thunders uttered their voices.

Moreover, this number hath much power; as in natural so in sacred cere-monial, and also in other things; therefore the seven days are related hither; also the seven planets, the seven stars called Pleiades, the seven ages of the world, the seven changes of man, the seven liberal arts, and as many mechanic̆, and so many forbidden; seven colours, seven metals, seven holes

in

in the head of a man, seven pair of nerves, seven mountains in the city of Rome, seven Roman kings, seven civil wars, seven wise men in the time of Jeremiah, seven wise men of Greece; also Rome did burn seven days by Nero; by seven kings were slain ten thousand martyrs : there were seven sleepers; and seven principal churches of Rome.

THE

THE SCALE OF

In the Original World,	Ararita,	אראדיהא		
In the Intelligible World,	צפקאיל Zaphiel,	צדקיאל Zadkiel,	כמאל Camael,	דפאל Raphael,
In the Celestial World,	שבתאי Saturn,	צרק Jupiter,	מאריס Mars,	שמש The Sun,
In the Elementary World,	The lapwing, The cuttle fish, The mole, Lead, The onyx,	The eagle, The dolphin, The hart, Tin, The saphire,	The vulture, The pike, The wolf, Iron, The diamond,	The swan, The sea calf, The lion, Gold, The carbuncle,
In the Lesser World,	The right foot, The right ear,	The head, The left ear.	The right hand, The right nostril,	The heart, The right eye,
In the Infernal World,	Hell, ניהבם	The gates of death, רצלתות	The shadow of death, ידעישחוס	The pit of destruction, באדישחת

THE NUMBER SEVEN.

Asser Eheie,	אשר אהיה		The name of God with seven letters.
האביאל Haniel,	מיבאל Michael,	נכריאל Gabriel ;	Seven angels which stand in the presence of God.
כונה Venus,	בוכב Mercury,	לבכה The Moon ;	Seven planets.
The dove, Thimallus, The goat, Copper, The emerald,	The stork, The mullet, The ape, Quicksilver, The achates,	The owl ; The sea cat ; Cat ; Silver ; Chrystal ;	Seven birds of the planets. Seven fish of the planets. Seven animals of the planets. Seven metals of the planets. Seven stones of the planets.
The privy members, , The left nostril,	The left hand, The mouth,	The left foot ; The left eye ;	Seven integral members distributed to the planets. Seven holes of the head distributed to the planets.
The Clay of death, טיטהיון	Perdition, אבוז	The depth of the earth, שאול	Seven habitations of infernals, which Rabbi Joseph of Castilia, the Cabalist, describes in the garden of nuts.

CHAP.

CHAP. XXIII.

OF THE NUMBER EIGHT, AND THE SCALE.

THE Pythagorians call Eight the number of justice, and fulness : first, because it is first of all divided into numbers equally even, viz. into four; and that division is, by the same reason, made into twice two, viz. twice two twice ; and by reason of this equality of division it took to itself the name of justice. But the other received the name of fulness, by reason of the contexture of the corporeal solidity, since the first makes a solid body. Hence that custom of Orpheus swearing by the eight deities, if at any time he would beseech Divine justice, whose names are these :---Fire, Water, Earth, the Heaven, Moon, Sun, Phanes, and the Night. There are only eight visible spheres of the heavens. Also, by it the property of corporeal nature is signified, which Orpheus comprehends in eight of his sea songs : this is also called the covenant, or circumcision, which was commanded to be done by the Jews the eighth day.

There were also, in the old law, eight ornaments of the priest, viz. a breastplate, a coat, a girdle, a mitre, a robe, an ephod, a girdle of the ephod, and a golden plate. Hither belongs the number to eternity, and the end of the world, because it follows the number seven, which is the mystery of time. Hence, also, the number of blessedness, as you may see in Matthew. It is also called the number of safety, and conservation; for there were so many souls of the sons of Jesse, from which David was the eighth.

THE

THE SCALE OF THE NUMBER EIGHT.

The name of God with eight letters,	Eloa Vadaath אלוה ודעת Jehova Vedaath יהוה ודעה								In the original world.
Eight rewards of the blessed,	Inheritance,	Incorruption,	Power,	Victory,	The vision of God,	Grace,	A kingdom,	Joy;	In the intelligible world.
Eight visible heavens,	The starry heaven,	The heaven of Saturn,	The heaven of Jupiter,	The heaven of Mars,	The heaven of the Sun,	The heaven of Venus,	The heaven of Mercury,	The heaven of the Moon;	In the celestial world.
Eight particular qualities,	The dryness of the earth,	The coldness of water,	The moisture of air,	The heat of fire,	The heat of air,	The moisture of water,	The dryness of fire,	The coldness of earth;	In the elementary world.
Eight kinds of blessed men,	The peace makers,	They that hunger and thirst after righteousness,	The meek,	They which are persecuted for righteousness sake,	Pure in heart,	Merciful,	Poor in spirit,	Mourners;	In the lesser world.
Eight punishments of the damned.	Prison,	Death,	Judgment,	The wrath of God,	Darkness,	Indignation,	Tribulation,	Anguish;	In the infernal world.

CHAP. XXIV.

OF THE NUMBER NINE, AND THE SCALE.

THERE are nine orders of blessed angels, viz. Seraphim, Cherubim, Thrones, Dominations, Powers, Virtues, Principalities, Archangels, and Angels, which Ezekiel figures out by nine stones, which are the sapphire, emerald, carbuncle, beryl, onyx, chrysolite, jasper, topaz, and sardis. This number hath also a great and occult mystery of the cross; for the ninth hour our Lord Jesus Christ breathed out his spirit. The astrologers also take notice of the number nine in the ages of men, no otherwise than they do of seven, which they call climac-terical years, which are eminent for some remarkable change. Yet sometimes it signifies imperfectness and incompleteness, because it does not attain to the perfection of the number ten, but is less by one, without which it is deficient, as Austin interprets it of the ten lepers. Neither is the longitude of nine cubits of Og, King of Basan, who is a type of the devil without a mystery.

THE

THE SCALE OF THE NUMBER NINE.

The name of God with nine letters,	Jehovah Sabboath, יהוה צבאוה			Jehovah Zidkenu, יהוהצרקבו			Elohim Gibor, אלוהים ניפוד			In the original world.
Nine quires of angels,	Seraphim,	Cherubim,	Thrones,	Dominations,	Powers	Virtues,	Principalities,	Archangels,	Angels ;	In the intelligible world.
Nine angels ruling the heavens,	Meratron,	Ophaniel,	Zaphkiel,	Zadkiel,	Camael	Raphael,	Haniel,	Michael,	Gabriel ;	
Nine moveable spheres,	The primum mobile,	The starry heaven,	The sphere of Saturn,	The sphere of Jupiter,	The sphere of Mars,	The sphere of the Sun,	The sphere of Venus,	The sphere of Mercury,	The sphere of the Moon;	In the celestial world.
Nine stones representing the nine quires of angels,	Saphire	Emerald,	Carbuncle,	Beryl,	Onyx,	Chrysolite,	Jasper,	Topaz,	Sardis ;	In the elementary world.
Nine senses, inward and outward together,	Memory,	Cogitative,	Imaginative,	Common sense,	Hearing,	Seeing,	Smelling,	Tasting,	Touching ;	In the lesser world.
Nine orders of devils,	False Spirits,	Spirits of lying,	Vessels of iniquity,	Avengers of wickedness,	Jugglers,	Airy Powers	Furies sowing mischief,	Sifters or triers,	Tempters, or ensnarers;	In the infernal world.

CHAP.

CHAP. XXV.

THE number Ten is called every number, or an univesal number, complete, signifying the full course of life; for beyond that we cannot number
but by replication; and it either implies all numbers within itself, or explains
them by itself, and its own, by multiplying them; wherefore it is accounted
to be of manifold religion and power, and is applied to the purging of souls.
Hence the antients called ceremonies Denary, because they were to be expiated
and to offer sacrifices, and were to abstain from some certain things for ten days.

There are ten sanguine parts of man : the menstrues, the sperm, the pla-
sonatic spirit, the mass, the humours, the organical body, the vegetative part,
the sensitive part, reason, and the mind.   There are, also, ten simple integral
parts constituting man : the bone, cartilage, nerve, fibre, ligament, artery,
vein, membrane, flesh, and skin.   There are, also, ten parts of which a man
consists intrinsically : the spirit, the brain, the lungs, the heart, the liver, the
gall, the spleen, the kidnies, the testicles, and the matrix.   There are ten
curtains in the temple, ten strings in the psaltery, ten musical instruments with
which the psalms were sung, the names whereof were---*neza*, on which their
odes were sung; *nablum*, the same as organs; *mizmor*, on which the Psalms;
sir, on which the Canticles; *tehila*, on which orations; *beracha*, on which be-
nedictions; *halel*, on which praises; *hodaia*, on which thanks; *asre*, on which
the felicity of any one; *hallelujah*, on which the praises of God only, and contemplations.   There were also ten singers of psalms, viz. *Adam, Abraham,
Melchisedeck, Moses, Asaph, David, Solomon*, and *the three sons of Chora*.
There are, also, ten commandments.   And then tenth day after the ascension
of Christ, the Holy Ghost came down.   Lastly, this is the number, in which
Jacob, wrestling with the Angel all night, overcame, and, at the rising of the
sun, was blessed, and called by the name of Israel.   In this number, Joshua
overcame thirty-one kings; and David overcame Goliah and the Philistines;
and Daniel escaped the danger of the lions.   This number is also circular, as
unity; because, being heaped together, returns into a unity, from whence it
had its beginning; and it is the end and perfection of all numbers, and the
                                                                    begin-

beginning of tens. As the number ten flows back into a unity, from whence it proceeded, so every thing that is flowing is returned back to that from which it had the beginning of its flux: so water returns to the sea, from whence it had its beginning; the body returns to the earth, from whence it was taken; time returns into eternity, from whence it flowed; the spirit shall return to God, who gave it; and, lastly, every creature returns to nothing, from whence it was created.* Neither is it supported but by the word of God, in whom all things are hid, and all things with the number ten, and by the number ten, make a round, as Proclus says, taking their beginning from God, and ending in him. God, therefore (that first unity, or one thing), before he communicated himself to inferiors, diffused himself first into the first of numbers, viz. the number three; then into the number ten, as into ten ideas and measures of making all numbers and all things, which the Hebrews call ten attributes, and account ten divine names; from which cause there cannot be a further number. Hence all tens have some divine thing in them, and in the law are required as his own, together with the first fruits, as the original of all things and beginning of numbers, and every tenth is as the end given to him, who is the beginning and end of all things.

SCALE OF THE NUMBER TEN.

---

* At the last, the elements give up what they have ever received; the sea gives up her dead, the fire gives up its fuel; the earth gives up the seminal virtue, &c.; and the air gives up whatever voice, sound, or impression it has received, so that not an oath, lie, or secret blasphemy, but what will appear as clear as noonday light at the great day of God.

THE

THE SCALE OF

In the original,	יהוהיהויהי The name of Jehovah of ten letters collected,			ואו הא The name of Jehovah of ten letters,	
	אהיה Eheie, כתר Kether,	ויהוה Jod Jehovah, חכמה Hochmah,	יהוהאלהים Jehovah Elohim, בינה Binah,	אל El, הכד Hesed,	אלהימניבר Elohim Gibor, גבורה Geburah,
In the intelli- gible world,	Seraphim, Hajothhakados, Merattron,	Cherubim, Orphanim, Jophiel,	Thrones, Aralim, Zaphkiel,	Dominations, Hasmallim, Zadkiel,	Powers, Seraphim, Camael,
In the celestial world,	Reschith hagalla-lim, the primum mobile,	Masloth, the sphere of the Zodiac,	Sabbathi, the sphere of Saturn,	Zedeck, the sphere of Jupiter,	Madim, the sphere of Mars,
In the element-ary world,	A dove,	A lizard,	A dragon,	An eagle,	A horse,
In the lesser world,	Spirit,	Brain,	Spleen,	Liver,	Gall,
In the infernal world,	False gods,	Lying spirits,	Vessels of iniquity.	Revengers of wickedness,	Jugglers,

THE NUMBER TEN.

יור הא Extended,		אלהימצבאות The name Elohim Sabaoth ;			The name of God with ten letters,
אליה Eloha, תפארת Tiphereth,	יחוהצבאות Jehovah Saboath, נצה Nezah,	אלהימצבאות Elohim Saboath, הוד Hod,	שרי Sadai, יסור Jesod,	אדני Adonai melech ; מלכות Malchuth ;	Ten names of God. Ten Sephiroth.
Virtues,	Principalities,	Archangels,	Angels,	Blessed souls ;	Ten orders of the blessed, according to Dionysius.
Malachim,	Elohim,	Ben Elohim,	Cherubim,	Issim ;	Ten orders of the blessed, according to the traditions of men.
Raphael,	Haniel,	Michael,	Gabriel,	The soul of Messiah ;	Ten angels ruling.
Schemes, the sphere of the Sun,	Noga, the sphere of Venus,	Cochab, the sphere of Mercury,	Levanah, the sphere of the Moon,	Holom Jesodoth, the sphere of the elements ;	Ten spheres of the world.
Lion,	Man,	The fox,	Bull,	Lamb ;	Ten animals consecrated to the gods.
Heart,	Kidnies,	Lungs,	Genitals,	Matrix ;	Ten parts intrinsical of man.
Airy powers,	Furies, the seminaries of evil,	Sifters, or triers,	Tempters, or ensnarers,	Wicked souls bearing rule ;	Ten orders of the damned.

CHAP.

CHAP. XXVI.

OF THE NUMBERS ELEVEN AND TWELVE, WITH THE CABALISTICAL SCALE.

THE number Eleven, as it exceeds number ten, which is the number of the commandments, so it falls short of the number Twelve, which is of grace and perfection; therefore it is called the number of sins, and the penitent. Now the number twelve is divine, and that whereby the celestials are measured;* it is, also, the number of signs in the Zodiac, over which there are

twelve

---

* The use of these Scales, in the composition of Talismans, Seals, Rings, &c., must be obvious to every student upon inspection, and are indispensably necessary to the producing of any effect whatever that the artist may propose to himself; for, as we have before observed, all things were formed according to the proportion of numbers, this seeming to be the principal pattern in the mind of the Creator; therefore, when at any time we set about any work or experiment in Celestial Magic, we are to have especial regard to the rule of numbers and proportions. For example, if we would obtain the celestial influence of any star, we are, first of all, to observe at what time that star is powerful in the heavens, I mean in good aspect with the benefices, and ruling in the day and hour appropriated to the planet, and in fortunate places of the figure; then we are to observe what divine names are ruling the intelligences, or spirits, to which the said planets are subject with their characters (which you may see at large in the Magical Tables of Numbers); then, by referring to the above Tables of the Scales, we may see, by inspection, to what numbers are attributed divine names, and, under them, the orders of the intelligences—the heavenly spheres—elements and their properties—animals, metals, and stones—powers of the soul—senses of man—virtues—the princes of the evil spirits—places of punishment—degrees of the damned souls—degrees of torments hereafter—and every thing that is either in heaven, or earth, or hell;—all our senses, motions, qualities, virtues, words, or works, are submitted to the proportions of numbers, as you may see fully exemplified in the different Scales of the Numbers; and all things that are knowable are demonstrable by them, and are attributed to them; therefore great is the knowledge and wisdom to be derived from numbers. Therefore the artist must be well acquainted with their virtues and properties—by them there is a way open for the knowing and understanding of all things; therefore let him diligently contemplate these Scales, and likewise what we have set down in our fourteenth and fifteenth Chapters preceding the Scales, where we have, upon good authority, explained sufficiently the extent and force of formal numbers, which ought to be well understood and attentively considered, as the ground and foundation of all our operations in this science, without which we are defrauded of the desired effect : therefore whenever we intend to set about any experiment, whether it be an image, or ring, or tablet, or mirror, or amulet, or any other instrument, we are to note first the site, order, number, and government of the intelligence and his planet, his measure of time, revolution in the heavens, &c.; likewise we are to engrave or write upon it its number, intelligence, or spirit, either for a good or bad effect, with the suitable characters and tables; likewise the effect desired, with the divine names congruent thereto; so that our operations may be strong, powerful, and suitable to the constellation and star, both in time, number, and proportion; with a due and attentive observation of all that we have written

concerning

twelve angels as chief, supported by the irrigation of the great name of God. In twelve years, also, Jupiter perfects his course; and the Moon daily runs through twelve degrees.   There are, also, twelve chief joints in the body of man, viz. in hands, elbows, shoulders, thighs, knees, and vertebræ of the feet.   There is, also, a great power of the number twelve in divine mysteries.   God chose twelve families of Israel, and set over them twelve princes; so many stones were placed in the midst of Jordan; and God commanded that so many should be set on the breast of the priest.   Twelve lions did bear the brazen sea that was made by Solomon; there were so many fountains in Helim; and so many Apostles of Christ set over the twelve tribes; and twelve thousand people were set apart and chosen.

concerning this, without which all our operations could never be brought to have the effect desired; and we are to mind that whenever such an instrument is perfected, that it is the more powerful when the planet or constellation (under which it was constructed) is ruling and potent in the Heavens; for at that time, whatever we desire to bring to perfection by the said Talisman, as a medium and instrument, shall by no means be prevented or hindered.   Therefore take this as a general rule, that all magical instruments whatsoever have no power in themselves, further than as they are formed under the influences, and according to the times and numbers of their proper stars and constellations; hence is derived the title we give this Book, viz. the *Constellatory Art*, or *Talismanic Magic*.   Those who would further consider the power, virtue, extent, and harmony of numbers, let them read Pythagoras, Plato, Averroena, Averroës, &c., who all agree in the virtues lying hid in numbers; and without the knowledge of which, no man can be a true philosopher.

THE SCALE OF

			הוא Holy,	בריר Blessed,	הקדש He,	
The names of God with twelve letters,						
The great name returned back into twelve banners,	יהוה	יההו	יוהה	הוהי	חויה	החיו
Twelve orders of blessed spirits,	Seraphim,	Cherubim,	Thrones,	Dominations,	Powers,	Virtues,
Twelve angels ruling over the twelve signs,	Malchidial,	Asmodel,	Ambriel,	Muriel,	Verchiel,	Hamaliel,
Twelve tribes,	Dan,	Ruben,	Judah,	Manasseh,	Asher,	Simeon,
Twelve prophets,	Malachi,	Haggai,	Zachariah,	Amos,	Hosea,	Micha,
Twelve apostles,	Matthias,	Thaddeus,	Simon,	John,	Peter,	Andrew,
Twelve signs of the Zodiac,	Aries,	Taurus,	Gemini,	Cancer,	Leo,	Virgo,
Twelve months,	March,	April,	May,	June,	July,	August,
Twelve plants,	Sang,	Upright vervain,	Bending vervain.	Comfrey,	Ladies' seal,	Calamint,
Twelve stones,	Sardonius,	A cornelian,	Topaz,	Calcedony,	Jasper,	Emerald,
Twelve principal members,	Head,	Neck,	Arms,	Breast,	Heart,	Belly,
Twelve degrees of the damned, and of devils.	False gods,	Lying spirits,	Vessels of iniquity,	Revengers of wickedness,	Jugglers,	Airy powers,

THE NUMBER TWELVE.

		אבבנזורותהקרש Father, Son, Holy Ghost.				In the original world.
והדי	יוהה	יהיה	היהו	היוה	ההוי	
Principalities,	Archangels,	Angels,	Innocents,	Martyrs,	Confessors.	In the intelligible world.
Zuriel,	Barbiel,	Adnachiel,	Hanael,	Gabriel,	Barchiel.	
Issachar,	Benjamin,	Naphthalin,	Gad,	Zabulon,	Ephraim.	
Jonah,	Obadiah,	Zephaniah,	Nahum,	Habakkuk,	Joel.	
Bartholomew,	Philip,	James the elder,	Thomas,	Matthew,	James the younger.	
Libra,	Scorpius,	Sagittarius,	Capricorn,	Aquarius,	Fisces.	In the celestial world.
September,	October,	November,	December,	January,	February.	In the elemental world
Scorpion grass,	Mugwort,	Pimpernel,	Dock,	Dragonwort,	Aristolochy.	
Beryl,	Amethyst,	Hyacinth,	Chrysophrasus,	Chrystal,	Sapphire.	
Kidnies,	Genitals,	Hams,	Knees,	Legs,	Feet.	In the elementary world.
Furies, the sowers of evil,	Sifters, or triers,	Tempters, or ensnarers,	Witches,	Apostates,	Infidels.	In the infernal world.

CHAP.

CHAP. XXVII.

OF THE NOTES OF THE HEBREWS AND CHALDEANS, AND OTHER NOTES OF MAGICIANS.

THE Hebrew characters have marks of numbers attributed to them far more excellent than any other language, since the greatest mysteries lie in the Hebrew letters, as is handled concerning these in that part of Cabala which we call Notariacon. Now the principal Hebrew letters are in number twenty-two, whereof five have various other certain figures in the end of a word, which, therefore, they call the five ending letters, which, being added to them aforesaid, make twenty-seven; which being then divided into three degrees, signify units, which are in the first degree---tens, which are in the second---and hundreds, which are in the third degree. Now every one, if they are marked with a great character, signifies so many thousands, as here----

3000	2000	1000
ג	ב	א

The classes of the Hebrew numbers are these which follow :----

9	8	7	6	5	4	3	2	1
ט	ח	ז	ו	ה	ד	ג	ב	א
90	80	70	60	50	40	30	20	10
צ	פ	ע	ס	נ	מ	ל	כ	י
900	800	700	600	500	400	300	200	100
ץ	ף	ן	ם	ך	ת	ש	ר	ק

Sometimes the final letters are not used, but we write thus :

1000	900	800	700	600	500
א	קתת	תת	שת	רת	קת

And by those simple figures, and by the joining them together, they describe all other compound numbers : as eleven, twelve, an hundred and ten, an hundred

hundred and eleven, by adding to the number ten those which are units; and in the like manner to the rest, after their manner; yet we describe the fifteenth number not by ten and five, but by nine and six, viz. וט; and that out of honour to the Divine name יה, which signifies fifteen, lest that sacred name should be abused to profane things. Likewise the Egyptians, Æthiopians, Chaldeans, and Arabians, have their marks of numbers, which serve for the making of magical characters; but the Chaldeans mark their numbers with the letters of their alphabet, after the manner of the Hebrews. I found, in a very antient book of Magic, some very elegant characters, which I have figured in the following manner :----

1	2	3	4	5	6	7	8	9

Now of these characters, turned towards the left hand, are made tens.

10	20	30	40	50	60	70	80	90

And those marks being downwards, to the right hand, make hundreds; to the left, thousands, viz.

100	200	300	400	500	600	700	800	900

1000	2000	3000	4000	5000	6000	7000	8000	9000

And

And by the composition and mixture of these characters, other compound numbers are most elegantly made, as you may perceive by these few :---

1510	1511	1471	1486	2421

1801

_____

CHAP. XXVIII.

THE MAGIC TABLES OF THE PLANETS----THEIR FORM AND VIRTUE----WHAT DIVINE NAMES,
INTELLIGENCES, AND SPIRITS, ARE SET OVER THEM.

THERE are certain magic tables of numbers distributed to the seven planets, which they call the sacred tables of the planets; because, being rightly formed, they are endued with many great virtues of the heavens, insomuch that they represent the divine order of the celestial numbers, impressed upon them by the *ideas* of the divine mind, by means of the soul of the world, and the sweet harmony of those celestial rays; signifying, according to proportion, supercelestial intelligences, which can no other way be expressed than by the marks of numbers, letters, and characters; for *material* numbers and figures can do nothing in the mysteries of hidden things, but representatively by *formal* numbers and figures, as they are governed and informed by intelligences and divine enumerations, which unite the extremes of the matter and spirit to the will of the elevated soul, receiving (through great affection, by the celestial power of the operator) a virtue and power from God, applied through the soul of the universe; and the observation of celestial constellations

to

Plate 1.

The Magic Tables Seals & Characters of the Planets their Intelligence & Spirits.

The Table of Saturn in his Compass

4	9	2
3	5	7
8	1	6

The same Table in Hebrew

ר	ט	ב
ג	ה	ז
ח	א	י

The Seal of Saturn 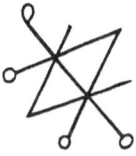 Of the Intelligence of ♄ Of the Spirit of ♄

The Table of Jupiter

4	14	15	1
9	7	6	12
5	11	10	8
16	2	3	13

In Hebrew

ר	יד	טו	א
ט	ז	ו	יב
ה	יא	י	ח
יו	ב	ג	יג

The Seal of Jupiter Of the Intelligence of ♃ Of the Spirit of ♃

The Table of Mars

11	24	7	20	3
4	12	25	8	16
17	5	13	21	9
10	18	1	14	22
23	6	19	2	15

In Hebrew

יא	כד	ז	כ	ג
ד	יב	כה	ח	יו
יז	ה	יג	כא	ט
י	יח	א	יד	כב
כג	ו	יט	ב	יה

The Seal of Mars 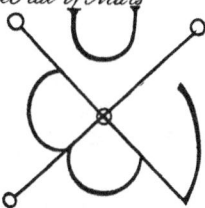 Of his Intelligence 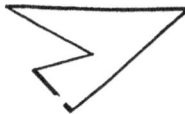 Of his Spirit

Designed by F. Barrett. Pub. by Lackington, Allen & Co. Engraved by R. Griffith.

The Magic Tables Seals & Characters of the Planets, their Intellegences & Spirits.

The Table of the Sun in his Compass

6	32	3	34	35	1
7	11	27	28	8	30
19	14	16	15	23	24
18	20	22	21	17	13
25	29	10	9	26	12
36	5	33	4	2	31

The same in Hebrew

The Character of the Seal of the Sun

His Intelligence

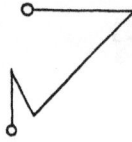

His Spirit

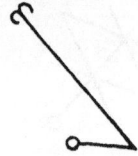

The Table of Venus in her Compass

22	47	16	41	10	35	4
5	23	43	17	42	11	29
30	6	24	49	81	36	12
13	31	7	25	43	19	37
38	14	32	1	26	44	20
21	39	8	33	2	27	45
46	15	40	9	34	3	28

in Hebrew

The Seal of Venus

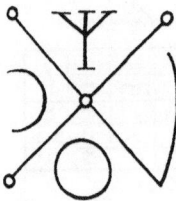

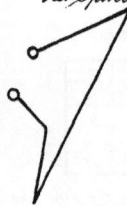

Her Intelligence

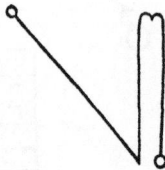

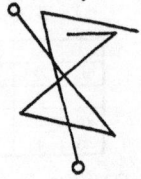

Her Spirit

Her Intelligences

F. Barrett Del.   Pub. by Lackington & Allen.   R.Griffith Sculp.

to a *matter* fit for a form, the mediums being disposed by the skill and industry of the magician.

But now we will hasten to explain each particular table.* The first table is assigned to the planet Saturn, and consists of a square of three, containing the particular numbers of nine, and in every line three every way, and through each diameter making fifteen---the whole sum of numbers forty-five; over this are set such divine names as fill up the numbers with an intelligence, to what is good, and a spirit to bad; and out of the same numbers are drawn the seal and character of Saturn, and of the spirits thereof, such as is beneath ascribed to the table.

Now this table being with a fortunate Saturn, engraven on a plate of lead, helps child-birth; and to make any man safe or powerful; and to cause success of petitions with princes and powers; but if it be done, Saturn being unfortunate, it hinders buildings, planting, and the like, and casts a man from honours and dignities, causes discord, quarrelling, and disperses an army.

The second is the table of Jupiter, which consists of a square drawn into itself; it contains sixteen particular numbers, and in every line and diameter four, making thirty-four; the sum of all is one hundred and thirty-six. There are over it divine names, with an intelligence to that which is good, and a spirit to bad; and out of it is drawn the character of Jupiter and the spirits thereof; if this is engraven on a plate of silver, with Jupiter being powerful and ruling in the heavens, it conduces to gain riches and favour, love, peace, and concord, and to appease enemies, and to confirm honours, dignities, and counsels; and dissolves enchantments if engraven on a coral.

The third table belongs to Mars, which is made of a square of five, containing twenty-five numbers, and of these, in every side and diameter, five, which makes sixty-five, and the sum of all is three hundred and twenty-five; and there are over it divine names with an intelligence to good, and a spirit to evil, and out of it is drawn the characters of Mars and of his spirits. These, with *Mars* fortunate, being engraven on an iron plate, or sword, makes

---

* For the figure of the Tables, Seals, Characters, &c. of the seven Planets, see the following Plates.

a man

a man potent in war and judgment, and petitions, and terrible to his enemies; and victorious over them; and if engraven upon the stone correola, it stops blood, and the menstrues; but if it be engraven, with *Mars* being unfortunate, on a plate of red brass, it prevents and hinders buildings---it casts down the powerful from dignities, honours, and riches---causes discord and hatred amongst men and beasts---drives away bees, pigeons, and fish---and hinders mills from working, *i. e.* binds them;---it likewise renders hunters and fighters unfortunate---causes barrenness in men and women---and strikes a terror into our enemies, and compels them to submit.

The fourth table is of the *Sun*, and is made of a square of six, and contains thirty-six particular numbers, whereof six in every side and diameter produce one hundred and eleven, and the sum of all is six hundred and sixty-six; there are over it divine names, with an intelligence to what is good, and a spirit to what is evil, and out of it is drawn the character of the Sun and of his spirits. This being engraven on a plate of pure gold, Sol being fortunate, renders him that wears it renowned, amiable, acceptable, potent in all his works, and equals him to a king, elevating his fortunes, and enabling him to do whatever he will. But with an unfortunate Sun, it makes one a tyrant, proud, ambitious, insatiable, and finally to come to an ill ending.

The fifth table is of Venus; consisting of a square of seven, drawn into itself, viz. of forty-nine numbers, whereof seven on each side and diameter make one hundred and seventy-five, and the sum of all is one thousand two hundred and twenty-five; there are, likewise, over it divine names, with an intelligence to good, and a spirit to evil; and there is drawn out of it the character of Venus, and her spirits. This being engraven on a plate of silver, Venus being fortunate, promotes concord, ends strife, procures the love of women, helps conception, is good against barrenness, gives ability for generation, dissolves enchantments, causes peace between man and woman, and makes all kinds of animals fruitful, and likewise cattle; and being put into a dove or pigeon house, causes an increase; it likewise drives away melancholy distempers, and causes joyfulness; and this being carried about travellers, makes

Plate 3.

The Magick Tables, Seals & Characters, of the Planets, their Intelligences & Spirits.

The Table of Mercury in his Compass.   The same in Hebrew

8	58	59	5	4	62	63	1
49	15	14	52	53	11	10	56
41	23	22	44	48	19	18	45
32	34	38	29	25	35	39	28
40	26	27	37	36	30	31	33
17	47	46	20	21	43	42	24
9	55	54	12	13	51	50	16
64	2	3	61	60	6	7	57

ח	נח	נט	ה	ד	סב	סג	א
מט	יה	יד	נב	נג	יא	י	נו
מא	כג	כב	מד	מה	יט	יח	מה
לב	לד	לח	כט	כה	לה	לט	כח
מ	כו	כז	לז	לו	ל	לא	לג
יז	מז	מו	כ	כא	מג	מב	כד
ט	נה	נד	יב	יג	נא	נ	יו
סד	ב	ג	סא	ס	ו	ז	נז

The Seal
or
Character
of
Mercury

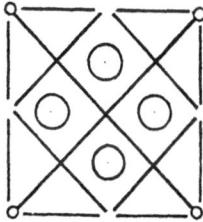

The Character
of the
Intelligence of Mercury

The Character
of the
Spirit of Mercury

Designed by F. Barrett 1801.   Pub. by Lackington Allen & Co.   Engraved by Bighton

The Magic Tables Seals & Characters of the Planets their Intelligences & Spirits

The Table of the Moon in her Compass

37	78	29	70	21	62	13	54	5
6	38	79	30	71	22	63	14	46
47	7	39	80	31	72	23	55	15
16	48	8	40	81	32	64	24	56
57	17	49	9	41	73	33	65	25
26	58	18	50	1	42	74	34	66
67	27	59	10	51	2	43	75	35
36	68	19	60	11	52	3	44	76
77	28	69	20	61	12	53	4	45

Table of the ☽ in Hebrew Notes

מה	יג	סב	כא	ע	כט	עה	לז	ה
מו	יד	סג	כב	עא	ל	עט	רח	ו
יה	נה	כו	נב	פ	רלא	עב	לג	מן
נו	כר	סד	רלב	פא	מח	הן	מה	יד
כה	סח	לג	אן	מאט	מט	יז	נן	נז
סו	לד	עה	גב	א	נ	יה	נה	כו
לה	עה	אמג	ב	נא	י	נשכז	פס	ז
עו	מר	ל	נב	יאס	טסחרלו	ג	מד	עו
מה	ר	גנ	יפכא	ל	כטסח	עז		

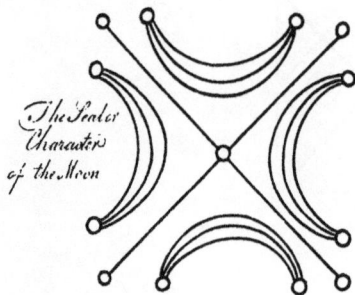

The Seal or Character of the Moon

Character of the Spirit of ☽

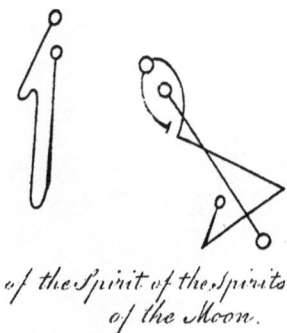

of the Spirit of the Spirits of the Moon.

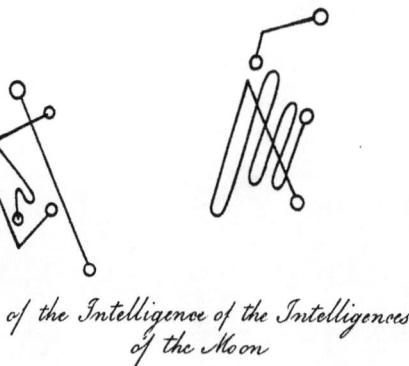

of the Intelligence of the Intelligences of the Moon

Barrett Del.   Pub. by Lackington & Allen.   R. Griffith.

makes them fortunate. But if it be formed upon brass, Venus being unfortunate, it acts contrary to all that has been said.

The sixth table is of Mercury, resulting from a square of eight drawn into itself, containing sixty-four numbers, whereof eight on every side and by both diameters make two hundred and sixty, and the sum of all is two thousand and eighty; and over it are set divine names, with an intelligence to good, with a spirit to bad, and from it is drawn a character of Mercury, and the spirits thereof; and if, with Mercury being fortunate, you engrave it upon silver, tin, or yellow brass, or write it upon virgin parchment, it renders the bearer thereof grateful, acceptable, and fortunate to do what he pleases : it brings gain, and prevents poverty; helps the memory, understanding, and divination, and to the understanding of occult things by dreams; but with an unfortunate Mercury does every thing contrary to this.

The seventh and last table is of the Moon : it consists of a square of nine, having eighty-one numbers in every side, and diameter nine, producing three hundred and sixty-nine; and the sum of all is three thousand three hundred and twenty-one.   There are over it divine names, with an intelligence to what is good, and a spirit to evil; and from it are drawn the characters of the Moon and the spirits thereof.   This, the Moon being fortunate, engraven on silver, makes the bearer amiable, pleasant, cheerful, and honoured, removing all malice and ill-will; it causes security in a journey, increase of riches, and health of body, drives away enemies, and other evil things from what place soever thou shalt wish them to be expelled.   But if the Moon be unfortunate, and it be engraven on a plate of lead, wherever it shall be buried it makes that place unfortunate, and the inhabitants thereabouts, as also ships, rivers, fountains, and mills ; and it makes every man unfortunate against whom it shall be directly done, making him fly his place of abode (and even his country) where it shall be buried ; and it hinders physicians and orators, and all men whatsoever in their office, against whom it shall be made.

Now how the seals and characters of the planets are drawn from these tables, the wise searcher, and he who shall understand the verifying of these tables, shall easily find out.

Book I.   Here

Here follow the divine names corresponding with the numbers of the planets, with the names of the intelligences and dæmons, or spirits, subject to those names.

It is to be understood that the intelligences are the presiding good angels that are set over the planets; but that the spirits or dæmons, with their names seals, or characters, are never inscribed upon any Talisman, except to execute any evil effect, and that they are subject to the intelligences, or good spirits; and again, when the spirits and their characters are used, it will be more conducive to the effect to add some divine name appropriate to that effect which we desire.

Names answering to the Numbers of Saturn.

ה

Numbers.	Divine Names.	Divine Names in Hebrew
3	Ab	אב
9	Hod	הד
15	Jah	יה
15	Hod	חוד
45	Jehovah extended	יורהאואוהא
45	Agiel, the Intelligence of Saturn	אגיאל
45	Zazel, the Spirit of Saturn	זאזל

Names answering to the Numbers of Jupiter.

24

4	Aba	אבא
16		הוה
16		אהי
34	El Ab	אלאב
136	Johphiel, the Intelligence of Jupiter	יהפיאל
136	Hismæl, the Spirit of Jupiter	הסמאל

Names answering to the Numbers of Mars.

♂

5	He, the letter of the holy name	ה
25		יהי
65	Adonai	ארני

Numbers

Numbers.	Divine Names.	Divine Names in Hebrew.
325	Graphiel, the Intelligence of Mars	גראפיאל
325	Barzabel, the Spirit of Mars	ברצאבאל

Names answering to the Numbers of the Sun.

☉

6	Vau, the letter of the holy name	ו
6	He extended, the letter of the holy name	הא
36	Eloh	אלה
111	Nachiel, the Intelligence of the Sun	נכיאל
666	Sorath, the Spirit of the Sun	סורה

Names answering to the Numbers of Venus.

♀

7	Aha	אהא
49	Hagiel, the Intelligence of Venus	הגיאל
175	Kedemel, the Spirit of Venus	קדמאל
1225	Bne Seraphim, the Intelligence of Venus	בני שרפים

Names answering to the Numbers of Mercury.

☿

8	Asboga, eight extended	אזבנה
64	Din	דין
64	Doni	דני
260	Tiriel, the Intelligence of Mercury	טיריאל
2080	Taphthartharath, the Spirit of Mercury	תפתרתרת

Names answering to the Numbers of the Moon.

☽

9	Hod	הד
81	Elim	אלים
369	Hasmodai, the Spirit of the Moon	השמודאי
3321	Schedbarschemoth Schartathan, the Spirit of the Spirits of the Moon	שרבשהמעאחשר תתו
3321	Malcha betharsisim hed beruah schehalim, the Intelligence of the Intelligences of the Moon	קלכאבתדשיסימסערברוחשהקים

CHAP.

CHAP. XXIX.

OF THE OBSERVATION OF THE CELESTIALS NECESSARY IN EVERY MAGICAL WORK.

EVERY natural virtue works things far more wonderful when it is not only compounded of a natural proportion, but also is informed by a choice observation of the celestials opportune to this (viz. when the celestial power is most strong to that effect which we desire, and also helped by many celestials), by subjecting inferiors to the celestials, as proper females, to be made fruitful by their males. Also, in every work there are to be observed the situation, motion, and aspect of the stars and planets, in signs and degrees, and how all these stand in reference to the length and latitude of the climate; for by this are varied the qualities of the angles, which the rays of the celestial bodies upon the figure of the thing describe, according to which celestial virtues are infused. So when you are working any thing which belongs to any planet, you must place it in its dignities fortunate, and powerful, and ruling in the day hour, and in the figure of the heavens. Neither must you expect the signification of the work to be powerful, but you must observe the Moon opportunely directed to this; for you shall do nothing without the assistance of the Moon. And if you have more patterns of your work, observe them all, being most powerful, and looking upon one another with a friendly aspect; and if you cannot have such aspects, it will be convenient at least that you take them angular. But you shall take the Moon either when she looks upon both, or is joined to one, and looks upon the other, or when she passes from the conjunction or aspect of one, to the conjunction or aspect of the other; for that, I conceive, must in no wise be omitted. Also, you shall in every work observe Mercury, for he is a messenger between the higher gods and the infernal gods: when he goes to the good, he increases their goodness---when to the bad, he hath influence on their wickedness. We call it an unfortunate sign or planet, when it is, by the aspect of Saturn or Mars especially, opposite or quadrant, for these are the aspects of enmity; but a conjunction, a trine, and a sextile aspect, are of friendship; between these there is a greater conjunction; but yet if you do already

behold

behold it through a trine, and the planet be received, it is accounted as already conjoined. Now all planets are afraid of the conjunction of the Sun, rejoicing in the trine, and sextile aspect thereof.

CHAP. XXX.

WHEN THE PLANETS ARE OF MOST POWERFUL INFLUENCE.

NOW we shall have the planets powerful when they are ruling in a house, or in exaltation, or triplicity, or term, or face, without combustion of what is direct in the figure of the heavens, viz. when they are in angles, especially of the rising, or tenth, or in houses presently succeeding, or in their delights; but we must take heed that they are not in the bounds or under the dominion of Saturn or Mars, lest they be in dark degrees, in pits, or vacuities. You shall observe that the angles of the ascendant, and tenth, and seventh be fortunate; as also the lord of the ascendant, and place of the Sun and Moon, and place of the part of fortune, and the lord thereof, the lord of the foregoing conjunction and prevention. But that they of the malignant planet fall unfortunate; unless happily they be significators of thy work, or can be of any advantage to thee, or in thy revolution or birth they had the predominance, for then they are not at all to be depressed. Now we shall have the Moon powerful if she be in her house, or exaltation, or triplicity, or face, or in degree convenient for the desired work; and if it hath a mansion of these twenty-eight, suitable to itself and the work, let her not in the way be burnt up,* nor slow in course---let her not be in the eclipse, or burnt by the Sun, unless she be in unity with the Sun---let her not descend in the southern latitude, when she goeth out of the burning---neither let her be opposite to the Sun, nor deprived of light---let her not be hindered by Mars or Saturn.

* Via Combusta.

CHAP.

CHAP. XXXI.

THERE is the like consideration to be had in all things concerning the fixed stars. Know this, that all the fixed stars are of the signification and nature of the seven planets; but some are of the nature of one planet, and some of two. Hence, as often as any planet is joined with any of the fixed stars of its own nature, the signification of that star is made more powerful, and the nature of the planet augmented; but if it be a star of two natures, the nature of that which shall be the stronger with it, shall overcome in signification: as for example, if it be of the nature of Mars and Venus, if Mars shall be the stronger with it, the nature of Mars shall overcome; but if Venus, the nature of Venus shall overcome. Now the natures of fixed stars are discovered by their colours, as they agree with certain planets, and are ascribed to them. Now the colours of the planets are these:---of Saturn, blue, and leaden, and shining with this; of Jupiter, citrine, near to a paleness, and clear with this; of Mars, red and fiery; of the Sun, yellow, and when it rises red, afterwards glittering; of Venus, white and shining---white in the morning, and reddish in the evening; of Mercury, glittering; of the Moon, fair. Know, also, that of the fixed stars, by how much the greater, and brighter, and apparent they are, so much the greater and stronger is the signification: such are those stars called by the astrologers of the first and second magnitude. I will tell thee some of these which are more potent to this faculty, viz. the navel of Andromeda, in the twenty-second degree of Aries, of the nature of Venus and Mercury---some call it jovial and saturnine; the head of Algol, in the eighteenth degree of Taurus, of the nature of Saturn and Jupiter; the Pleiades are also in the twenty-second degree, a lunary star by nature, and complexion martial; also Aldeboram, in the third degree of Gemini, is of the nature of Mars, and complexion of Venus---but Hermes places this in the twenty-fifth degree of Aries; the Goat star, in the thirteenth degree of Gemini, is of the nature of Jupiter and Saturn; the Great Dog star is in the seventh degree of Cancer and Venereal;

the

the Little Dog star is in the seventeenth degree of the same, and is of the nature of Mercury, and complexion of Mars; the King star, which is called the Heart of the Lion, is in the twenty-first degree of Leo, and of the nature of Jupiter and Mars; the tail of the Great Bear is in the nineteenth degree of Virgo, and is venereal and lunary. The star which is called the Right Wing of the Crow, is in the seventh degree of Libra; and in the thirteenth degree of the same, is the left wing of the same, and both of the nature of Saturn and Mars. The star called Spica, is in the sixteenth degree of the same, and is venereal and mercurial. In the seventeenth degree of the same is Alcameth, of the nature of Mars and Jupiter; but of this, when the Sun's aspect is full towards it---of that, when on the contrary. Elepheia, in the fourth degree of Scorpio, of the nature of Venus and Mars. The heart of the Scorpion is in the third degree of Sagittarius, of the nature of Mars and Jupiter. The falling Vulture is in the seventh degree of Capricorn, temperate, mercurial, and venereal. The tail of Capricorn is in the sixteenth degree of Aquarius, of the nature of Saturn and Mercury. The star called the Shoulder of the Horse, is in the third degree of Pisces, of the nature of Jupiter and Mars.---And it shall be a general rule for you to expect the proper gifts of the stars, whilst they rule---to be prevented of them, they being unfortunate, as is above shewed; for celestial bodies, inasmuch as they are affected fortunately or unfortunately, so much do they affect us, our works, and those things which we use, fortunately or unhappily. And although many effects proceed from the fixed stars, yet they are attributed to the planets; as because being more near to us, and more distinct and known, so because they execute whatever the superior stars communicate to them.

CHAP.

CHAP. XXXII.

OF THE SUN AND MOON, AND THEIR MAGICAL CONSIDERATIONS.

THE Sun and Moon have obtained the administration of ruling the heavens, and all bodies under the heavens. The Sun is the lord of all elementary virtues; and the Moon, by virtue of the Sun, is mistress of generation, increase or decrease. Albumsar says, that by the Sun and Moon, life is infused into all things; which Orpheus calls the enlivening eyes of Heaven. The Sun giveth light to all things of itself, and gives it plentifully, not only to all things in heaven and air, but earth and deep. Whatever good we have, Jamblicus says, we have it from the Sun alone; or from it through other things. Heraclitus calls the Sun, the fountain of celestial light; and many of the Platonists placed the soul of the world chiefly in the Sun, as that which, filling the whole globe of the Sun, doth send forth its rays on all sides, as it were a spirit through all things, distributing life, sense, and motion to the universe. Hence the antient naturalists called the Sun the very heart of Heaven; and the Chaldeans put it as the middle of the Planets. The Egyptians also placed it in the middle of the world, viz. between the two fives of the world; i. e. above the Sun they place five planets, and under him, the Moon and four elements. For it is, amongst the other stars, the image and statue of the great Prince of both worlds, viz. terrestrial and celestial; the true light, and the most exact image of God himself: whose essence resembles the Father---light, the Son---heat, the Holy Ghost. So that the Platonists have nothing to hold forth the divine essence more manifestly by than this. The Sun disposes even the very spirit and mind of man, which Homer says, and is approved by Aristotle, that there are in the mind such like motions as the Sun, the prince and moderator of the planets, brings to us every day; but the Moon, the nearest to the earth, the receptacle of all the heavenly influences, by the swiftness of her course, is joined to the Sun, and the other planets and stars, every month; and receiving the beams and influences of all the other planets and stars, as a conception, bringing them forth to the inferior world, as being next to itself; for all the

stars

stars have influence on it, being the last receiver, which afterwards communicates the influence of all the superiors to these inferiors, and pours them forth
on the earth; and it more manifestly disposes these inferiors than others.
Therefore her motion is to be observed before the others, as the parent of all
conceptions, which it diversely issues forth in these inferiors, according to the
diverse complexion, motion, situation, and different aspects to the planets and
other stars; and though it receives powers from all the stars, yet especially
from the Sun, as oft as it is in conjunction with the same, it is replenished
with vivifying virtue; and, according to the aspect thereof, it borrows its
complexion. From it the heavenly bodies begin that series of things which
Plato calls the golden chain; by which every thing and cause, being linked
one to another, do depend on the superior, even until it may be brought unto
the supreme cause of all, from which all things depend; hence it is, that,
without the Moon intermediating, we cannot at any time attract the power of
the superiors; therefore, to obtain the virtue of any star, take the stone and
herb of that planet, when the Moon fortunately comes under, or has a good
aspect on, that star.

CHAP. XXXIII.

OF THE TWENTY-EIGHT MANSIONS OF THE MOON, AND THEIR VIRTUES.

AND seeing the Moon measures the whole space of the Zodiac in the time
of twenty-eight days, hence it is that the wise men of the *Indians*, and most
of the antient astrologers have granted twenty-eight mansions to the Moon,
which, being fixed in the eighth sphere, do enjoy (as *Alpharus* says) divers
names and properties, from the various signs and stars which are contained in
them; through which, while the Moon wanders, it obtains many other powers
and virtues; but every one of these mansions, according to the opinion of
Abraham, contained twelve degrees, and fifty-one minutes, and almost twenty-

BOOK I.   six

six seconds, whose names, and also their beginnings in the Zodiac, of the eighth sphere, are these :---The first is called *Alnath;* that is, the horns of Aries : his beginning is from the head of Aries, of the eighth sphere : it causes discords and journies. The second is called *Allothaim,* or *Albochan ;* thas is, the belly of Aries ; and his beginning is from the twelfth degree of the same sign, fifty-one minutes, twenty-two seconds complete : it conduces to the finding of treasures, and to the retaining captives. The third is called *Achaomazon,* or *Athoray ;* that is, showering, or Pleiades : his beginning is from the twenty-fifth degree of Aries complete, forty-two minutes, and fifty-one seconds ; it is profitable to sailors, huntsmen, and alchymists. The fourth mansion is called *Aldebaram,* or *Aldelamen ;* that is, the eye or head of Taurus : his beginning is from the eighth degree of Taurus, thirty-four minutes and seventeen seconds of the same, Taurus being excluded : it causes the destruction and hindrances of buildings, fountains, wells, gold mines, the flight of creeping things, and begets discord. The fifth is called *Alchatay,* or *Albachay;* the beginning of it is after the twenty-first degree of Taurus, twenty-five minutes, forty seconds : it helps to the return from a journey, to the instruction of scholars ; it confirms edifices, it gives health and good-will. The sixth is called *Athanna,* or *Alchaya ;* that is, the little star of great light : his beginning is after the fourth degree of Gemini, seventeen minutes, and nine seconds ; it conduces to hunting and besieging towns, and revenge of princes : it destroys harvest and fruits, and hinders the operation of the physician. The seventh is called *Aldimiach,* or *Alarzach ;* that is, the arm of Gemini, and begins from the seventeenth degree of Gemini, eight minutes, and thirty-four seconds, and lasts even to the end of the sign ; it confirms gain and friendship ; it is profitable to lovers, and destroys magistracies : and so is one quarter of the heaven completed in these seven mansions, and in the like order and number of degrees, minutes, and seconds ; the remaining mansions, in every quarter, have their several beginnings ; namely, so that in the first sign of this quarter three mansions take their beginnings ; in the other two signs, two mansions in each ; therefore the seven following mansions begin with Cancer, whose names are *Alnaza Anatrachya ;* that is, misty or cloudy, viz. the eighth mansion ;

mansion; it causes love, friendship, and society of fellow travellers: it drives away mice, and afflicts captives, confirming their imprisonment. After this is the ninth, called *Archaam*, or *Arcaph*; that is, the eye of the Lion: it hinders harvest and travellers, and puts discord between men. The tenth is called *Algtlioche*, or *Albgebh*; that is, the neck or forehead of Leo: it strengthens buildings, promotes love, benevolence, and help against enemies. The eleventh is called *Azobra*, or *Ardaf*; that is, the hair of the lion's head: it is good for voyages, and gain by merchandise, and for redemption of captives. The twelfth is called *Alzarpha*, or *Azarpha*; that is the tail of Leo: it gives prosperity to harvest and plantations, but hinders seamen; and is good for the bettering of servants, captives, and companions. The thirteenth is named *Alhaire*; that is, Dog stars, or the wings of Virgo: it is prevalent for benevolence, gain, voyages, harvests, and freedom of captives. The fourteenth is called *Achureth*, or *Arimet*; by others, *Azimeth*, or *Athumech*, or *Alcheymech*; that is, the spike of Virgo, or flying spike: it causes the love of married folks; it cures the sick, is profitable to sailors, but hinders journies by land; and in these the second quarter of the heaven is completed. The other seven follow: the first of which begins in the head of Libra, viz. the fifteenth mansion, and its name is *Agrapha*, or *Algrapha*; that is, covered, or covered flying: it is profitable for extracting treasures, for digging of pits, it assists divorce, discord, and destruction of houses and enemies, and hinders travellers. The sixteenth is called *Azubene*, or *Ahubene*; that is, the horns of Scorpio: it hinders journies and wedlock, harvest and merchandise; it prevails for redemption of captives. The seventeeth is called *Alchil*; that is, the crown of Scorpio: it betters a bad fortune, makes love durable, strengthens buildings, and helps seamen. The eighteenth is called *Alchas*, or *Altob*; that is, the heart of Scorpio: it causes, discord, sedition, conspiracy against princes and mighty ones, and revenge from enemies; but it frees captives, and helps edifices. The nineteenth is called *Allatha*, or *Achala*; by others, *Hycula*, or *Axala*; that is, the tail of Scorpio: it helps in besieging of cities, and taking of towns, and in the driving of men from their places, and for the destruction of seamen and perdition of captives. The twentieth is called *Abnahaya*; that is, a beam:

it

it helps for the taming of wild beasts, for strengthening of prisons; it destroys the wealth of societies; it compels a man to come to a certain place. The twenty-first is called *Abeda*, or *Albeldach*, which is a desert: it is good for harvest, gain, buildings, and travellers, and causes divorce; and in this is the third quarter of heaven completed. There remains the seven last mansions completing the last quarter of Heaven: the first of which, being in order to the twenty-second, beginning from the head of Capricorn, called *Sadahacha*, or *Zodeboluch*, or *Zandeldena;* that is, a pastor: it promotes the flight of servants and captives, that they may escape; and helps the curing of diseases. The twenty-third is called *Zabadola*, or *Zobrach;* that is, swallowing: it is for divorce, liberty of captives and health to the sick. The twenty-fourth is called *Sadabath*, or *Chadezoad;* that is, the star of fortune: it is prevalent for the benevolence of married people, for the victory of soldiers; it hurts the execution of government, and prevents its being exercised. The twenty-fifth is called *Sadalabra*, or *Sadalachia;* that is, a butterfly, or a spreading forth: it favours besieging and revenge; it destroys enemies, and causes divorce; confirms prisons and buildings, hastens messengers; it conduces to spells against copulation, and so binds every member of man that it cannot perform its duty. The twenty-sixth is called *Alpharg*, or *Phragal Mocaden;* that is, the first drawing: it causes union, health of captives, destroys building and prisons. The twenty-seventh is called *Alchara Alyhalgalmoad*, or the second drawing: it increases harvests, revenues, gain, and heals infirmities, but hinders buildings, prolongs prisons, causes danger to seamen, and helps to infer mischiefs on whom you shall please. The twenty-eighth and last is called *Albotham*, or *Alchalcy;* that is, Pisces: it increases harvest and merchandise; it secures travellers through dangerous places; it makes for the joy of married people; but it strengthens prisons, and causes loss of treasures. And in these twenty-eight mansions lie hid many secrets of the wisdom of the antients, by which they wrought wonders on all things which are under the circle of the Moon; and they attributed to every mansion his resemblances, images, and seals, and his president intelligences, and worked by the virtue of them after different manners.

                                                                        CHAP.

CHAP. XXXIV.

HOW SOME ARTIFICIAL THINGS (AS IMAGES, SEALS, AND SUCH LIKE) MAY OBTAIN SOME
VIRTUE FROM THE CELESTIAL BODIES.

SO great is the extent, power, and efficacy of the celestial bodies, that not only natural things, but also artificial, when they are rightly exposed to those above, do presently suffer by that most potent agent, and obtain a wonderful life. The magicians affirm, that not only by the mixture and application of natural things, but also in images, seals, rings, glasses, and some other instruments, being opportunely framed under a certain constellation, some celestial illustrations may be taken, and some wonderful thing may be received; for the beams of the celestial bodies being animated, living, sensual, and bringing along with them admirable gifts, and a most violent power, do, even in a moment, and at the first touch, imprint wonderful powers in the images, though their matter be less capable. Yet they bestow more powerful virtues on the images if they be framed not of any, but of a certain matter, namely, whose natural, but also specifical virtue is agreeable with the work, and the figure of the image is like to the celestial; for such an image, both in regard to the matter naturally congruous to the operation and celestial influence, and also for its figure being like to the heavenly one, is best prepared to receive the operations and powers of the celestial bodies and figures, and instantly receives the heavenly gift into itself; though it constantly worketh on another thing, and other things yield obedience to it.

CHAP.

CHAP. XXXV.

OF THE IMAGES OF THE ZODIAC----WHAT VIRTUES, THEY BEING ENGRAVEN, RECEIVE
FROM THE STARS.

BUT the celestial images, according to whose likeness images of this kind
are framed, are many in the heavens; some visible and conspicuous, others
only imaginary, conceived and set down by the *Egyptians, Indians,* and
Chaldeans; and their parts are so ordered, that even the figures of some of
them are distinguished from others; for this reason they place in the circle
of the Zodiac twelve general images, according to the number of the signs;
of these, they constituting Aries, Leo, and Sagittarius, for the fiery and oriental
triplicity, report that it is profitable against fevers, palsy, dropsy, gout, and
all cold and phlegmatic infirmities; and that it makes him who carries it to
be acceptable, eloquent, ingenious and honourable; because they are the
houses of Mars, Sol, and Jupiter. They made, also, the image of a lion
against melancholy phantasies, dropsy, plague and fevers, and to expel
diseases; at the hour of the Sun, the first degree of the sign Leo ascending,
which is the face and decanate of Jupiter; but against the stone, and diseases
of the reins, and against hurts of beasts, they made the same image when Sol,
in the heart of the lion, obtained the midst of heaven. And again, because
Gemini, Libra, and Aquarius, do constitute the ærial and occidental triplicity,
and are the houses of Mercury, Venus, and Saturn, they are said to put to
flight diseases, to conduce to friendship and concord, to prevail against melancholy, and to cause health; and they report that Aquarius especially frees
from the quartan. Also, that Cancer, Scorpio, and Pisces, because they constitute the watery and northern triplicity, do prevail against hot and dry fevers,
also against the hectic, and all choleric passions; but Scorpio, because among
the members it respects the privy parts, doth provoke to lust; but these did
frame it for this purpose, his third face ascending, which belongs to Venus;
and they made the same, against serpents and scorpions, poisons and evil
spirits, his second face ascending, which is the face of the Sun, and decanate of

Jupiter;

Geomantic Characters.

Figure				Planets
	Via	*Populus*		☾
	Conjunctio			☿
	Albus			
	Amissio			♀
	Puella			
	Fortuna Major	*Fortuna Minor*		☉
	Reubus	*Puer*		♂
	Aquisitio			♃
	Lætitia			♃
	Carcer	*Tristitia*		♄
Dragon's Head	*Caput Dragonis*			☊
Dragon's Tail	*Cauda Dragonis*			☋

Jupiter; and they report that it maketh him who carries it wise, of a good colour; and they say that the image of Cancer is most efficacious against serpents and poison, when Sol and Luna are in conjunction in it, and ascend in the first and third face; for this is the face of Venus, and the decanate of Luna; but the second face of Luna the decanate of Jupiter. They report, also, that serpents are tormented when the Sun is in Cancer; also, that Taurus, Virgo, and Capricorn, because they constitute the earthly and southern triplicity, do cure hot infirmities, and prevail against the synocal fever; it makes those who carry it grateful, acceptable, eloquent, devout and religious; because they are the houses of Venus, Mars, and Saturn, Capricorn also is reported to keep men in safety, and also places in security, because it is the exaltation of Mars.

CHAP. XXXVI.

OF THE IMAGES OF SATURN.

BUT now what images they did attribute to the planets. Although of these things very large volumes have been written by the antient wise men, so that there is no need to declare them here, notwithstanding I will recite a few of them; for they made, from the operations of Saturn, *Saturn* ascending in a stone, which is called the load-stone, the image of a man, having the countenance of a hart, and camel's feet, and sitting upon a chair or else a dragon, holding in his right hand a scythe, in his left a dart, which image they hoped would be profitable for prolongation of life; for Albumasar, in his book *Sadar*, proves that Saturn conduces to the prolongation of life; where, also, he says that certain regions of India being subject to Saturn, there men are of a very long life, and die not unless by extreme old age. They made, also, an image of Saturn, for length of days, in a sapphire, at the hour of Saturn, *Saturn* ascending or fortunately constituted; whose figure was an old man sitting upon a high chair, having his hands lifted up above his head,

and

and in them holding a fish or sickle, and under his feet a bunch of grapes, his head covered with a black or dusky coloured cloth, and all his garments black or dark. They also make this same image against the stone, and diseases of the kidnies, viz. in the hour of Saturn, *Saturn* ascending with the third face of Aquarius. They made also, from the operations of Saturn, an image for the increasing of power, Saturn ascending in Capricorn; the form of which was an old man leaning on a staff, having in his hand a crooked sickle, and clothed in black. They also made an image of melted copper, Saturn ascending in his rising, viz. in the first degree of Aries, or the first degree of Capricorn; which image they affirm to speak with a man's voice. They made also, from the operations of Saturn, and also Mercury, an image of cast metal, like a beautiful man, which, they said, would foretel things to come; and made it on the day of Mercury, on the third hour of Saturn, the sign of Gemini ascending, being the house of Mercury, signifying prophets; Saturn and Mercury being in conjunction in Aquarius, in the ninth house of heaven, which is also called God. Moreover, let Saturn have a trine aspect on the ascendant, and the Moon in like manner, and the Sun have an aspect on the place of conjunction; Venus, obtaining some angle, may be powerful and occidental; let Mars be combust by the Sun, but let it not have an aspect on Saturn and Mercury; for they said that the splendour of the powers of these stars was diffused upon this image, and it did speak with men, and declare those things which are profitable for them.

CHAP. XXXVII.
OF THE IMAGES OF JUPITER.

FROM the operations of Jupiter they made, for prolongation of life, an image in the hour of Jupiter, Jupiter being in his exaltation fortunately ascending, in a clear and white stone; whose figure was a man crowned
clothed

clothed with garments of a saffron colour, riding upon an eagle or dragon, having in his right hand a dart, about, as it were, to strike it into the head of the same eagle or dragon. They made, also, another image of Jupiter, at the same convenient season, in a white and clear stone, especially in crystal; and it was a naked man crowned, having both his hands joined together and lifted up, as it were, deprecating something sitting in a four-footed chair, which is carried by four winged boys; and they affirm that this image increases felicity, riches, honours, and confers benevolence and prosperity, and frees from enemies. They made, also, another image of Jupiter, for a religious and glorious life, and advancement of fortune; whose figure was a man having the head of a lion or a ram, and eagle's feet, and clothed in saffron coloured clothes.

CHAP. XXXVIII.
OF THE IMAGES OF MARS.

FROM the operations of Mars, they made an image in the hour of Mars (Mars ascending in the second face of Aries), in a martial stone, especially in a diamond; the form of which was a man armed, riding upon a lion, having in his right hand a naked sword erect, carrying in his left hand the head of a man. They report that an image of this kind renders a man powerful in good and evil, so that he shall be feared by all; and whoever carries it, they give him the power of enchantment, so that he shall terrify men by his looks when he is angry, and stupify them. They made another image of Mars, for obtaining boldness, courage, and good fortune, in wars and contentions; the form of which was a soldier, armed and crowned, girt with a sword, carrying in his right hand a long lance; and they made this at the hour of Mars, the first face of Scorpio ascending with it.

Book I.   CHAP.

CHAP. XXXIX.

OF THE IMAGES OF THE SUN.

FROM the operations of the Sun they made an image at the hour of the Sun, the first face of Leo ascending with the Sun; the form of which was a king crowned, sitting in a chair, having a raven in his bosom, and under his feet a globe: he is clothed in saffron coloured clothes. They say that this image renders men invincible and honourable, and helps to bring their business to a good end, and to drive away vain dreams; also to be prevalent against fevers, and the plague; and they made it in a balanite stone, or a ruby, at the hour of the Sun, when he, in his exaltation, fortunately ascends. They made another image of the Sun in a diamond, at the hour of the Sun ascending in his exaltation; the figure of which was a woman crowned, with the gesture of one, dancing and laughing, standing in a chariot drawn by four horses, having in her right hand a looking-glass or buckler, in the left a staff, leaning on her breast, carrying a flame of fire on her head. They say that this image renders a man fortunate, and rich, and beloved of all; and they made this image on a cornelian stone, at the hour of the Sun ascending in the first face of Leo, against lunatic passions, which proceed from the combustion of the Moon.

CHAP. XL.

OF THE IMAGES OF VENUS.

FROM the operations of Venus they made an image, which was available for favour and benevolence, at the very hour it ascended into Pisces; the form of which was the image of a woman, having the head of a bird, the feet of an eagle, and holding a dart in her hand. They made another image of Venus,

to

to obtain the love of women, in the lapis lazuli, at the hour of Venus, *Venus* ascending in *Taurus;* the figure of which was a naked maid, with her hair spread abroad, having a looking-glass in her hand, and a chain tied about her neck---and near her a handsome young man, holding her with his left hand by the chain, but with his right hand doing up her hair, and both looking lovingly on one another---and about them is a little winged boy, holding a sword or dart. They made another image of Venus, the first face of *Taurus, Libra,* or *Pisces,* ascending with Venus; the figure of which was a little maid, with her hair spread abroad, clothed in long and white garments, holding a laurel apple, or flowers, in her right hand, in her left a comb : it is said to make men pleasant, jocund, strong, cheerful, and to give beauty.

CHAP. XLI.
OF THE IMAGES OF MERCURY.

FROM the operations of Mercury they made an image of Mercury, Mercury ascending in Gemini ; the form of which was a handsome young man, bearded, having in his left hand a rod, round which a serpent was entwined---in the right he carried a dart; having his feet winged. They say that this image confers knowledge, eloquence, diligence in merchandise, and gain ; moreover, to obtain peace and concord, and cure fevers. They made another image of Mercury, ascending in Virgo, for good will, wit, and memory ; the form of which was a man sitting upon a chair, or riding on a peacock, having eagle's feet, and on his head a crest, and in his left hand holding a cock of fire.

CHAP

CHAP. XLII.

OF THE IMAGES OF THE MOON.

FROM the operations of the Moon they made an image for travellers against weariness, at the hour of the Moon, the *Moon* ascending in its exaltation; the figure of which was a man leaning on a staff, having a bird on his head, and a flourishing tree before him. They made another image of the Moon for the increase of the fruits of the earth, and against poisons, and infirmities of children, at the hour of the Moon, it ascending in the first face of Cancer; the figure of which was a woman cornuted, riding on a bull, or a dragon with seven heads or a crab, and she hath in her right hand a dart, in her left a looking glass, clothed with white or green, and having on her head two serpents with horns twined together, and to each arm a serpent twined about, and to each foot one in like manner. And thus much spoken concerning the figures of the planets, may suffice.

CHAP. XLIII.

OF THE IMAGES OF THE HEAD AND TAIL OF THE DRAGON OF THE MOON.

THEY made, also, the image of the head and tail of the Dragon of the Moon, namely, between an aerial and fiery circle, the likeness of a serpent, with the head of a hawk, tied about them after the manner of the great letter Theta; they made it when Jupiter, with the head, obtained the mid heaven; which image they affirm to avail much for the success of petitions, and would signify by this image a good and fortunate genius, which they would represent by this image of the serpent; for the Egyptians and Phoenicians do extol this creature above all others, and say it is a divine creature, and hath a divine nature; for in this is a more acute spirit, and a greater fire than in any other, which thing is manifest both by his swift motion without feet, hands,

or

or any other instruments ; and also that it often renews its age with his skin, and becomes young again ; but they made the image of the tail like as when the Moon was eclipsed in the tail, or ill affected by Saturn or Mars, and they made it to introduce anguish, infirmity, and Misfortune : we call it an evil genius.

THE TALISMAN OF THE DRAGON's HEAD.

CHAP. XLIV.
OF THE IMAGES OF THE MANSIONS OF THE MOON.

THEY made, also, images for every mansion of the Moon as follows :----

In the first, for the destruction of some one, they made, in an iron ring, the image of a black man, in a garment of hair, and girdled round, casting a small lance with his right hand : they sealed this in black wax, and perfumed it with liquid storax, and wished some evil to come.

In the second, against the wrath of the prince, and for reconciliation with him, they sealed, in white wax and mastich, the image of a king crowned, and perfumed it with lignum aloes.

In the third, they made an image in a silver ring, whose table was square ; the figure of which was a woman, well clothed, sitting in a chair, her right hand being lifted up on her head ; they sealed it, and perfumed it with musk, camphire, and calamus aromaticus. They affirmed that this gives happy fortune, and every good thing.

In the fourth, for revenge, separation, enmity, and ill-will, they sealed, in red wax, the image of a soldier sitting on a horse, holding a serpent in his right hand : they perfumed it with red myrrh and storax.

In the fifth, for the favour of kings and officers, and good entertainment, they sealed, in silver, the head of a man, and perfumed it with red sanders.

In the sixth, to procure love between two, they sealed, in white wax, two images, embracing one another, and perfumed them with lignum aloes and amber.

In the seventh, to obtain every good thing, they sealed, in silver, the image of a man, well clothed, holding up his hands to Heaven, as it were, praying and supplicating, and perfumed it with good odours.

In the eighth, for victory in war, they made a seal in tin, being an image of an eagle, having the face of a man, and perfumed it with brimstone.

In the ninth, to cause infirmities, they made a seal of lead, being the image of a man wanting his privy parts, covering his eyes with his hands; and they perfumed it with rosin of the pine.

In the tenth, to facilitate child bearing, and to cure the sick, they made a seal of gold, being the head of a lion, and perfumed it with amber.

In the eleventh, for fear, reverence, and worship, they made a seal of a plate of gold, being the image of a man riding on a lion, holding the ear thereof in his left hand, and in his right holding forth a bracelet of gold; and they perfumed it with good odours and saffron.

In the twelfth, for the separation of lovers, they made a seal of black lead, being the image of a dragon fighting with a man; and they perfumed it with the hairs of a lion, and assafœtida.

In the thirteenth, for the agreement of married people, and for dissolving of all the charms against copulation, they made a seal of the images of both (of the man in red wax, and the woman in white), and caused them to embrace one another; perfuming it with lignum aloes and amber.

In the fourteenth, for divorce and separation of the man from the woman, they made a seal of red copper, being the image of a dog biting his tail; and they perfumed it with the hair of a black dog and a black cat.

In the fifteenth, to obtain friendship and good will, they made the image of a man sitting, and inditing letters, and perfumed it with frankincense and nutmegs.

In

In the sixteenth, for gaining much merchandising, they made a seal of silver, being the image of a man, sitting on a chair, holding a balance in his hand; and they perfumed it with well smelling spices.

In the seventeenth, against thieves and robbers, they sealed with an iron seal the image of an ape, and perfumed it with the air of an ape.

In the eighteenth, against fevers and pains of the belly, they made a seal of copper, being the image of a snake with his tail above his head; and they perfumed it with hartshorn; and said this same seal put to flight serpents, and all venomous creatures, from the place where it is buried.

In the nineteenth, for facilitating birth, and provoking the menstrues, they made a seal of copper, being the image of a woman holding her hands upon her face; and they perfumed it with liquid storax.

In the twentieth, for hunting, they made a seal of tin, being the image of Sagittary, half a man and half a horse; and they perfumed it with the head of a wolf.

In the twenty-first, for the destruction of some body, they made the image of a man, with a double countenance before and behind; and they perfumed it with brimstone and jet, and put it in a box of brass, and with it brimstone and jet, and the hair of him whom they would hurt.

In the twenty-second, for the security of runaways, they made a seal of iron, being the image of a man, with wings on his feet, bearing a helmet on his head; and they perfumed it with *argent vive*.

In the twenty-third, for destruction and wasting, they made a seal of iron, being the image of a cat, having a dog's head; and they perfumed it with dog's hair taken from the head, and buried it in the place where they intended the hurt.

In the twenty-fourth, for multiplying herds of cattle, they took the horn of a ram, bull, or goat, or of that sort of cattle they would increase, and sealed in it, burning, with an iron seal, the image of a woman giving suck to her son; and they hanged it on the neck of that cattle who was the leader of the flock, or they sealed it in his horn.

In

In the twenty-fifth, for the preservation of trees and harvest, they sealed, in the wood of a fig tree, the image of a man planting ; and they perfumed it with the flowers of the fig tree, and hung it on the tree.

In the twenty-sixth, for love and favour, they sealed, in white wax and mastich, the figure of a woman washing and combing her hair ; and they perfumed it with good odours.

In the twenty-seventh, to destroy fountains, pits, medicinal waters, and baths, they made, of red earth, the image of a man winged, holding in his hand an empty vessel, and perforated ; and the image being burnt, they put in the vessel assafœtida and liquid storax, and they buried it in the pond or fountain which they would destroy.

In the twenty-eighth, for getting fish together, they made a seal of copper, being the image of a fish ; and they perfumed it with the skin of a sea fish, and cast it into the water where they would have the fish gathered.

Moreover, together with the aforesaid images, they wrote down also the names of the spirits, and their characters, and invoked and prayed for those things which they pretended to obtain.

CHAP. XLV.

THAT HUMAN IMPRECATIONS NATURALLY IMPRESS THEIR POWERS UPON EXTERNAL THINGS----AND HOW MAN'S MIND, THROUGH A DEGREE OF DEPENDENCIES, ASCENDS INTO THE INTELLIGIBLE WORLD, AND BECOMES LIKE TO THE MORE SUBLIME SPIRITS AND INTELLIGENCES.

THE celestial souls send forth their virtues to the celestial bodies, which transmit them to this sensible world ; for the virtues of the terrene orb proceed from no other cause than celestial. Hence the magician, that will work by them, uses a cunning invocation of the superiors, with mysterious words and a certain kind of ingenious speech, drawing the one to the other ; yet by a natural force, through a certain mutual agreement between them, whereby

things

things follow of their own accord, or sometimes are drawn unwillingly. Hence says Aristotle, in his sixth book of his Mystical Philosophy, "that when any one, by binding or bewitching, calls upon the Sun or other stars, praying them to assist the work desired, the Sun and other stars do not hear his words; but are moved, after a certain manner, by a certain conjunction and mutual series, whereby the parts of the world are mutually subordinate the one to the other, and have a mutual consent, by reason of their great union : as in a man's body, one member is moved by perceiving the motion of another; and in a harp, one string is moved by the motion of another. So when any one moves any part of the world, other parts are moved by the perceiving of that motion."---The knowledge, therefore, of the dependency of things following one the other, is the foundation of all wonderful operation, which is necessarily required to the exercising the power of attracting superior virtues. Now the words of men are certain natural things; and because the parts of the world mutually draw one the other; therefore a magician invocating by words, works by powers fitted to Nature, by leading some by the love of one to the other; or drawing others, by reason of the one following after the other; or by repelling, by reason of the enmity of one to the other, from the contrariety and difference of things, and multitude of virtues; which, although they are contrary and different, yet perfect one part. Sometimes, also, he compels things by way of authority, by the celestial virtue, because he is not a stranger to the heavens. A man, therefore, if he receives the impression of a ligation, or fascination, doth not receive it according to the rational soul, but sensual; and if he suffers in any part, he suffers according to the animal part; for they cannot draw a knowing and intelligent man by reason, but by receiving that impression and force by sense; inasmuch as the animal spirit of man is, by the influence of the celestials, and co-operation of the things of the world, affected beyond his former and natural disposition. As the son moves the father to labour, although unwilling, to keep and maintain him, although he be wearied; and the desire to rule, is moved by anger and other labours to get the dominion; and the indigency of nature, and fear of poverty, moves a man to desire riches; and the ornaments and beauty of women, is an incite-

BOOK I.   ment

ment to concupiscence ; and the harmony of a wise musician moves his hearers
with various passions, whereof some do voluntary follow the consonancy of art,
others conform themselves by gesture, although unwilling, because their sense
is captivated, their reason not being intent to these things.   Hence they fall
into errors, who think those things to be above nature, or contrary to nature---
which indeed are by nature, and according to nature.   We must know, therefore, that every superior moves its next inferior, in its degree and order, not
only in bodies, but also in spirits : so the universal soul moves the particular
soul ; the rational acts upon the sensual, and that upon the vegetable ; and
every part of the world acts upon another, and every part is apt to be moved
by another.   And every part of this inferior world suffers from the heavens,
according to their nature and aptitude, as one part of the animal body suffers for another.   And the superior intellectual world moves all things below
itself; and, after a manner, contains all the same beings, from the first to the
last, which are in the inferior world.   Celestial bodies, therefore, move the
bodies of the elementary world, compounded, generable, sensible (from the
circumference to the centre), by superior, perpetual, and spiritual essences, depending on the primary intellect, which is the acting intellect ; but upon the
virtue put in by the word of God ; which word the wise Chaldeans of Babylon
call, the Cause of Causes ; because from it are produced all beings : the acting
intellect, which is the second, from it depends ; and that by reason of the
union of the word with the First Author, from whom all things being are truly
produced : the word, therefore, is the image of God---the acting intellect, the
image of the word---the soul is the image of this intellect---and our word is
the image of the soul, by which it acts upon natural things naturally, because
nature is the work thereof.   And every one of those perfects his subsequent : as
a father his son ; and none of the latter exists without the former ; for they are
depending among themselves by a kind of ordinate dependency---so that when
the latter is corrupted, it is returned into that which was next before it, until
it come to the heavens ; then to the universal soul ; and, lastly, into the acting
intellect, by which all other creatures exist ; and itself exists in the principal
author, which is the creating word of God, to which, at length, all things are
                                                                        returned.

returned. Our soul, therefore, if it will work any wonderful thing in these inferiors, must have respect to their beginning, that it may be strengthened and illustrated by that, and receive power of acting through each degree, from the very first Author. Therefore we must be more diligent in contemplating the souls of the stars---then their bodies, and the super-celestial and intellectual world---then the celestial, corporeal, because that is more noble; although, also, this be excellent, and the way to that, and without which medium the influence of the superior cannot be attained to. As for example: the Sun is the king of stars, most full of light; but receives it from the intelligible world, above all other stars, because the soul thereof is more capable of intelligible splendour. Wherefore he that desires to attract the influence of the Sun, must contemplate upon the Sun; not only by the speculation of the exterior light, but also of the interior. And no man can do this, unless he return to the soul of the Sun, and become like to it, and comprehend the intelligible light thereof with an intellectual sight, as the sensible light with the corporeal eye; for this man shall be filled with the light thereof, and the light whereof, which is an under type impressed by the supernal orb, it receives into itself; with the illustration whereof his intellect being endowed, and truly like to it, and being assisted by it, shall at length attain to that supreme brightness, and to all forms that partake thereof; and when he hath received the light of the supreme degree, then his soul shall come to perfection, and be made like to spirits of the Sun, and shall attain to the virtues and illustrations of the supernatural virtue, and shall enjoy the power of them, if he has obtained faith in the First Author. In the first place, therefore, we must implore assistance from the First Author; and praying, not only with mouth, but a religious gesture and supplicant soul, also abundantly, incessantly, and sincerely, that he would enlighten our mind, and remove darkness, growing upon our souls by reason of our bodies.

CHAP.

CHAP. XLVI.

THE CONCLUSION OF THE CONSTELLATORY PRACTICE, OR TALISMANIC MAGIC; IN WHICH IS INCLUDED THE KEY OF ALL THAT HAS BEEN WRITTEN UPON THIS SUBJECT; SHEW-ING THE PRACTICE OF IMAGES, &c. BY WAY OF EXAMPLE, AND LIKEWISE THE NECES-SARY OBSERVATIONS OF THE CELESTIALS, TOWARDS THE PERECTION OF TALISMANICAL OPERATIONS.

WE will now shew thee the observations of celestial bodies, which are re-quired for the practice of these things, which are briefly as follow :----

To make any one fortunate, we make an image at that time in which the *significator of life, the giver of life,* or *Hylech, the signs and planets,* are fortunate : let the ascendant and mid-heaven, and the lords thereof, be fortunate ; and also the place of the Sun and Moon ; part of fortune and lord of conjunction or prevention, make before their nativity, by depressing the malignant planets, *i.e.* taking the times when they are depressed. But if we would make an image to procure misery, we must do contrary to this; and those which we before placed fortunate, we must now make unfortunate, by taking the malignant stars when they rule. And the same means we must take to make any place, region, city, or house unfortunate. But if you would make any one unfortunate who hath injured you, let there be an image made under the ascension of that man whom thou wouldst make unfortunate ; and thou shalt take, when unfortunate, the lord of the house of his life, the lord of the ascendant and the Moon, the lord of the house of the Moon, the lord of the house of the lord ascending, and the tenth house and the lord thereof. Now, for the building, success, or fitting of any place, place fortunes in the ascendant thereof; and in the first and tenth, the second and eighth house, thou shalt make the lord of the ascendant, and the lord of the house of the Moon, for-tunate. But to chase away certain animals (from any place) that are noxious to thee, that they may not generate or abide there, make an image under the ascension of that animal which thou wouldst chase away or destroy, and after the likeness thereof; for instance, now, suppose thou wouldst wish to chase away scorpions from any place : let an image of a scorpion be made, the sign

Scorpio

Scorpio ascending with the Moon ; then thou shalt make unfortunate the ascendant, and the lord thereof, and the lord of the house of *Mars ;* and thou shalt make unfortunate the lord of the ascendant in the eighth house ; and let them be joined with an aspect malignant, as opposite or square, and write upon the image the name of the ascendant, and of the lord thereof, and the Moon, the lord of the day and hour ; and let there be a pit made in the middle of the place from which thou wouldst drive them, and put into it some earth taken out of the four corners of the same place, then bury the image there, with the head downwards, saying---" This is the burying of the *Scorpions*, that they may be forced to leave, and come no more into this place."---And so do by the rest.

Now for gain, make an image under the ascendant of that man to whom thou wouldst appoint the gain ; and thou shalt make the lord of the second house, which is the house of substance, to be joined with the lord of the ascendant, in a trine or sextile aspect, and let there be a reception amongst them ; thou shalt make fortunate the eleventh, and the lord thereof, and the eighth ; and, if thou canst, put part of fortune in the ascendant or second ; and let the image be buried in that place, or from that place, to which thou wouldst appoint the gain or fortune. Likewise, for agreement or love, let be made an image in the day of Jupiter, under the ascendant of the nativity of him whom you would wish to be beloved ; make fortunate the ascendant and the tenth, and hide the evil from the ascendant ; and you must have the lords of the tenth, and planets of the eleventh, fortunate, joined to the lord of the ascendant, from the trine or sextile, with reception ; then proceed to make another image, for him whom thou wouldst stir up to love ; whether it be a friend, or female, or brother, or relation, or companion of him whom thou wouldst have favoured or beloved, if so, make an image under the ascension of the eleventh house from the ascendant of the first image ; but if the party be a wife, or a husband, let it be made under the ascension of the seventh ; if a bro- ther, sister, or cousin, under the ascension of the third house ; if a mother, of the tenth, and so on :---now let the significator of the ascendant of the second image be joined to the significator of the ascendant of the first, and let there

be

be between them a reception, and let the rest be fortunate, as in the first image; afterwards join both the images together in a mutual embrace, or put the face of the second to the back of the first, and let them be wrapped up in silk, and cast away or spoiled.

Also, for the success of petitions, and obtaining of a thing denied, or taken, or possessed by another, make an image under the ascendant of him who petitions for the thing; and cause the lord of the second house to be joined with the lord of the ascendant, from a trine or sextile aspect, and let there be a reception betwixt them ; and, if it can be so, let the lord of the second be in the obeying signs, and the lord of ascendant in the ruling : make fortunate the ascendant and the lord thereof; and beware that the lord of the ascendant be not retrograde, or combust, or cadent, or in the house of opposition, *i. e.* in the seventh from his own house; let him not be hindered by the malignant planets, but let him be strong and in an angle; thou shalt make fortunate the ascendant, and the lord of the second, and the Moon : and make another image for him that is petitioned to, and begin it under the ascendant belonging to him : as if he is a king, or prince, &c. begin it under the ascendant of the tenth house from the ascendant of the first image; if a father, under the fourth ; if a son, under the fifth, and so of the like; then put the significator of the second image, joined with the lord of the ascendant of the first image from a trine or sextile, and let him receive it; and put them both strong and fortunate, without any hinderance ; make all evil fall from them ; thou shalt make fortunate the tenth and the fourth, if thou canst, or any of them; and when the second image shall be perfect, join it with the first, face to face, and wrap them in clean linen, and bury them in the middle of his house who is the petitioner, under a fortunate significator, *the fortune being strong;* and let the face of the first image be towards the north, or rather towards that place where the thing petitioned for doth remain ; or, if it happens that the petitioner goes forward to obtain the thing desired or petitioned for, let him carry the said images with him. Thus we have given, in a few examples, the key of all Talismanical operations whatsoever, by which wonderful effects may be wrought either by images, by rings, by glasses, by seals, by tables, or any

other

Magick Seals, or Talismans.

No. 1.   No. 2.   No. 3.

The Seal of Saturn   Seal of Jupiter   Seal of Mars

Lead   Silver   Iron

No. 4.   No. 5.   No. 6

Seal of the Sun   Seal of Venus   Seal of Mercury

Pure Gold   Copper   Silver & Tin

Designed by F. Barret   Engraved by R. Griffith

Pub. by Lackington Allen & Co

9 781585 090310